Father, Son, and Holy Spirit: Relationshi
plishment of one of the finest scholars
sentation to a pastors' conference, B
scholars can never do. He has written
literate layman can understand. Finally, we have a volume that reaches beyond the academic community and into the life of the local church.

—PAIGE PATTERSON, President
Southwestern Baptist Theological Seminary

Thanks to the clear thinking and biblically solid perspective of my friend, Bruce Ware, we are now blessed with this stimulating and edifying description of our God who is worthy of wonder and awe. Here is a theology that will launch your heart in worship—as all good theology should!

—JOSEPH M. STOWELL, President
Moody Bible Institute

Many automatically equate theology with complexity and even irrelevancy. Nothing could be further from the truth. Dr. Ware has the rare gift of making the profound accessible; he understands why theology matters and that it is the basis for true doxology.

—NANCY LEIGH DEMOSS, author, host of
Revive Our Hearts radio program

With all of the material available on the doctrine of the Trinity, I am thrilled to finally have a resource that will help the person in the pew understand how to properly articulate the doctrine and also grasp why it matters. Bruce Ware has brilliantly demonstrated that the manner in which the members of the Trinity relate to one another has a direct impact on marriage, parenting, work relationships, and more. His book is a great combination of theological precision and pastoral application. Pastors should make sure their members are familiar with this work.

—RANDY STINSON
Executive Director, CBMW

The truth that God is three equal yet different manifestations of one nature is at the very heart of the Christian faith. Knowing God means knowing him as Father, Son, and Holy Spirit. Furthermore, the truine God created male and female in his image. He intends that his very nature be expressed in human relationships. The doctrine of the Trinity thus has enormous implications for our everyday lives. This book will help you behold God's wondrous beauty and undestand how it can be reflected in the way you interact with others. It is both awe-inspiring and immensely practical. If you think that theology is boring or irrelevant, you haven't read Bruce Ware. Ware does a mastrful job of helping the ordinary person understand and apply this important doctrine.

—MARY KASSIAN, author and speaker,
Alabaster Flask Ministries

FATHER, SON, AND HOLY SPIRIT

FATHER, SON,

RELATIONSHIPS, ROLES, & RELEVANCE

& HOLY SPIRIT

BRUCE A. WARE

CROSSWAY BOOKS
WHEATON, ILLINOIS

Father, Son, and Holy Spirit: Relationships, Roles, and Relevance

Copyright © 2005 by Bruce A. Ware

Published by Crossway Books
  a publishing ministry of Good News Publishers
  1300 Crescent Street
  Wheaton, Illinois 60187

All rights reserved. No part of this publication may be reproduced, stored in a retrieval system, or transmitted in any form by any means, electronic, mechanical, photocopy, recording, or otherwise, without the prior permission of the publisher, except as provided by USA copyright law.

Cover design: Jon McGrath

First printing 2005

Printed in the United States of America

Scripture quotations are from *The Holy Bible, English Standard Version*®, copyright © 2001 by Crossway Bibles, a publishing ministry of Good News Publishers. Used by permission. All rights reserved.

Library of Congress Cataloging-in-Publication Data
Ware, Bruce A.
    Father, Son, and Holy Spirit : relationships, roles, and relevance
/ Bruce A. Ware.
        p. cm.
    Includes bibliographical references and index.
    ISBN 13: 978-1-58134-668-8 (tpb)
    ISBN 10: 1-58134-668-9
    1. Trinity. I. Title.
BT111.3.W37   2005
231'.044—dc22   200402768

VP   18   17   16   15   14   13   12
16   15   14   13   12   11   10   9   8

To my beloved parents,
William A. and Ruth M. Ware,
in deep appreciation for their nurture, instruction, and love,
and for introducing me to the true and living God whom I,
with them, love so dearly.

CONTENTS

ACKNOWLEDGMENTS

It is the rare pastors' conference that requests its speaker to devote five one-hour sessions to the doctrine of the Trinity. But such was the case. I am very grateful to the Conservative Baptist Northwest team who invited me out to Sun River, Oregon, March 2004, to speak at their annual meetings, giving me the opportunity to develop the talks that I've since rewritten and developed into this book. Mark Hoeffner, Dave Cetti, and Luke Hendrix worked with me in structuring the talks, and they explained so well to those gathered why it would be beneficial that we devote these meetings to a study "Beholding the Wonder of the Trinity." I thought then, and continue to believe, that if the leadership of our churches and denominations had the kind of theological vision shown by this leadership team in the CBNW office, our churches would benefit greatly. More than any other need we have as human beings and as Christians, we need to know God. So, I am deeply grateful for their vision and for the opportunity to share such glorious truths with eager and hungry pastors and wives.

I owe a special debt of thanks to my secretary, Mrs. Keri Forrest, who painstakingly transcribed my taped messages from the CBNW meetings, allowing me an invaluable starting place for writing this book. And my sincere thanks is also extended to Marvin Padgett and Bill Deckard of Crossway Books. Mr. Deckard labored diligently to improve this work. Readers will never know how much clearer and smoother it is, but they too can be grateful for his skill and competence.

Finally, as always, my family has supported me much through the process of developing the original messages for the CBNW annual meetings, and throughout the writing of this book. Jodi and Rachel at home, and Bethany away at college, have loved me and prayed for me much, and for them I am deeply grateful. I also wish to give special thanks to my own parents, Bill and Ruth Ware, to whom this book is dedicated. I had less difficulty growing up than some have had in knowing the "fatherhood" of God because of the godly parenting by these choice servants of his. Their love and prayer support for me is priceless, and I hope they know how much I love them.

Above all, I give praise, honor, and thanksgiving to the glorious triune God, of whom this book so inadequately endeavors to speak. The older I get, and the more I grow as a Christian, the more astonished I am with the greatness and majesty that is God's alone. My deepest desire is that he will be pleased with the efforts here. For all that rightly speaks of God, I freely and gladly give to God all the glory, and for all that misses the mark, I pray for his forgiveness and correction. God alone is worthy, and so to him be all praise and worship, both now and forevermore.

I

BEHOLDING THE WONDER OF OUR TRIUNE GOD: IMPORTANCE OF THIS DOCTRINE

INTRODUCING GOD TO THOSE WHO KNOW HIM

Why should we devote our time and attention to a study of the Trinity? While many answers can be given, and several will be provided later in this chapter, I'll begin with one primary answer: would God have chosen to reveal himself to us as the one God who is Father, Son, and Holy Spirit, unless he knew that this would be important to our understanding of him and of our faith? Must it not be the case that God cares greatly that we "get it," that we see him for who he is? And must it not matter to our own lives whether or not we understand him as the triune God that he is?

By analogy, what would a husband think if his wife said to him, "You know, there's something about me that is very near and dear to my heart that you don't know, something that I've tried to tell you in the past but you just haven't gotten it; you haven't paid attention or listened when I've talked about it. And it really matters both to me and to our relationship that you understand this. But it isn't the easiest thing to understand. I'm asking you, 'Will you listen? Will you let me share with you something very,

very important to understanding who I am, something that can make a big difference in the quality of our relationship with each other?'"

Perhaps God would say something similar about his revelation of his triune nature. He might say, "There is something about me that I've told you, but it is something that you've just not been interested in understanding. To be sure, it isn't the easiest thing to understand, but it matters, and I really care that you see this. I am one God, but I am also three. I am one God only as I am Father, Son, and Holy Spirit, and this makes a difference in how you see me and how we relate with one another. This matters in terms of how I do my work, who I am eternally, and how I have made you. I've told you about this in my Word, but you haven't yet seen the beauty and wonder of what I've said. So now, will you listen to something I care about very dearly and deeply, and will you take it to heart?"

It is my hope and prayer that, through this study, we will be able to hear the voice of the Lord helping us to understand the beauty and glory of the God whom we already know as God. But do we know him as we should? Do we know him as he truly is? We will explore, then, what he has to tell us about his triune nature; his eternal existence; his work in his created order; the way he manifests himself as Father, Son, and Holy Spirit; and what this means for our lives. I trust that this will be a rich and deeply rewarding study, and that we will see how relevant and applicable the doctrine of the Trinity is to our own lives. Yes, our understanding of who God really is, and our understanding of how this affects our lives and ministries—both of these areas can be greatly enlarged through looking more carefully at something God cares much about: that he is the one God who is Father, Son, and Holy Spirit.

The focus of our study of the Trinity will be to examine especially the ways in which the Father, Son, and Holy Spirit *relate to one another,* how they *relate to us,* and what *difference this makes in our lives.* If you've shied away from this doctrine, fearing that it is just too complicated or mysterious, I would encourage you to look again. Without question, there are aspects of the doctrine of the Trinity that are beyond our comprehension, but since God has deemed it good and right to reveal to us what he has about how the Father, Son, and Holy Spirit relate and work, we must endeavor to understand what he's told us. And the glorious thing is that as we look more carefully at this triune nature and see better how the Persons of the Godhead relate within the Trinity and with us, we will discover a whole new vista of practical application that has the potential of greatly enriching our own lives. So for the sake of understanding God as he is, and for the sake of experiencing the richness of these truths in application to our lives and ministries, I propose that we see what we can learn about the triune God.

Here are ten additional reasons why understanding the Trinity is important and beneficial to our lives as Christians. As we consider these, I believe we'll see both the deepened understandings that await us, and the growth in our relationships with God and others that can occur by seeing God better for who he is—the one God who is only one as he is also the three Persons of the Father, the Son, and the Holy Spirit.

TEN REASONS TO FOCUS ON THE WONDER OF THE TRINITY

Why should we devote the time and effort needed to think carefully about the triune nature of God? Consider these ten reasons, and marvel at the glory of God manifested as triune.

1. The doctrine of the Trinity is one of the *most important distinguishing doctrines* of the Christian faith and therefore is deserving of our careful study, passionate embrace, and thoughtful application.

As one considers the distinctiveness of Christianity compared to other religious traditions and ideas, clearly the doctrine of the Trinity not only distinguishes the Christian faith from all others, it also establishes the basis for all that we hold dear as Christian believers. This doctrine shows us in essential and glorious ways what it is to be "Christian." To know the Christian faith, and to know what it means to be a Christian, one must see more clearly what it means for God to be triune.

More personally, I believe that many Christian people will one day stand before the Lord aware as never before that they spent too little time getting to know the depth and the wonder of who God really is—including his revelation of himself as Father, Son, and Holy Spirit, the one God over all. If we are to know God rightly, we must know him as he is, as he has revealed himself. And this means knowing him as the one God who is the triune Father, Son, and Holy Spirit.

Christians down through the ages who have known God testify of the beauty, glory, and wonder that they have come to see in him as the triune God. How enriched our lives can be, and how much more joyful our experience and fruitful our service, when informed by an intimate knowledge of who God is. Let us press on, then, to know with greater clarity the one God who is Father, Son, and Holy Spirit. This distinguishing doctrine of our faith is crucial to the Christian faith itself, and it is rich, wondrous, and fully deserving of our careful attention and joyful embrace.

2. The doctrine of the Trinity is both *central and necessary for the Christian faith* to be what it is. Remove the Trinity, and the whole Christian faith disintegrates.

Can the Christian faith survive, as it were, if the doctrine of the Trinity is omitted? Are we aware of just how crucial this doctrine is to all else we believe as Christians? As one ponders this question, it becomes clear that the work of God (e.g., creation, redemption, consummation) can be rightly understood only as the work of the Father, Son, and Holy Spirit unified in the purpose of the work but distinct in the participation and contribution of each member. To illustrate the significance of the Trinity to our faith, consider just briefly the relation of the doctrine of the Trinity to the Christian understanding of salvation. In order for us sinners to be saved, one must see God at one and the same time as the one judging our sin (the Father), the one making the payment of infinite value for our sin (the divine Son), and the one empowering and directing the incarnate—human—Son so that he lives and obeys the Father, going to the cross as the substitute for us (the Holy Spirit). The Christian God, to be savior, must then be Father, Son, and Holy Spirit. That is, our salvation comes as the Father judges our sin in his Son, who became incarnate and lived his life in the power of the Spirit as the perfect and sinless God-man, and accomplished his perfect obedience to the Father through the power of the Spirit. Disregard the Trinity and you necessarily undermine salvation. More can be said, but this example is sufficient to demonstrate how crucial this doctrine is to the whole of our faith as Christians.

3. *Worship* of the true and living God consciously acknowledges the relationship and roles of Father, Son, and Holy Spirit.

As Paul demonstrates in Ephesians 1:3-14, the whole of God's work is accomplished in a trinitarian framework, and hence the worship of this God—the true and living God who is Father, Son, and Holy Spirit—necessarily requires a conscious understanding and honoring of the Trinity. The very opening of Paul's praise of God here sets out Christian worship in trinitarian terms. He begins, "Blessed be the *God and Father* of our *Lord Jesus Christ,* who has blessed us *in Christ* with every *spiritual blessing* in the heavenly places."[1] In light of verses 13 and 14, where Paul focuses on the gift of the Spirit, who mediates to us the blessings of Christ's work, it seems clear that the "spiritual blessings" of verse 3 are really blessings of the Spirit, given to us by the Father, in his Son. Paul is saying that praise to God must be given to God the Father, through the Son, in light of his blessings being mediated to us by his Spirit. So here we have in one verse the praise of God, who is none other than Father, Son, and Holy Spirit. Christian worship recognizes this reality and order. Thus Christian worship is inherently trinitarian.

4.   The Christian's life of *prayer* must rightly acknowledge the roles of Father, Son, and Spirit as we pray to the Father, through the Son, in the power of the Spirit.

Recall for a moment the opening line of Jesus' instruction regarding how we should pray. "Pray then like this," he said. "Our *Father* in heaven, hallowed be your name." May I suggest something both clear and radical? If Jesus taught us to pray to the Father, then we ought to do this. For one reason or another, we sometimes follow a different practice. We may encourage our children, especially, to open their prayers with, "Dear Jesus," despite the fact that Jesus said to pray "Our Father in heaven . . ." Perhaps we do not think about prayer as we should because we do not understand the doctrine of the Trinity. As Jesus taught us, we should pray to the Father through the Son. Jesus Christ is the mediator. He is the one through whom we address the Father. He is the one who brings us access to the Father. Our prayers bring spiritual benefit only when we pray in his name. And prayers that bring fruit in the kingdom are those offered in the power of the Spirit. We pray as the Spirit prompts and urges us to pray. So prayer rightly understood—Christian prayer—is prayer to the Father, through the Son, in the power of the Spirit. To pray aright, we need a deep appreciation for the doctrine of the Trinity.

5. The Christian's *growth in Christlikeness or sanctification* is rightly understood and enriched when seen as the work of the triune God.

In Christian sanctification, the full work of the triune Persons is involved, together in harmonious unity, but each with his distinctive contribution. First, the Father ordains and secures our holiness. As noted above in Ephesians 1, we are to give praise first and foremost to the Father, since "he chose us in him [Christ] before the foundation of the world, that we should be holy and blameless before him" (Eph. 1:4). This ordained plan then moves toward becoming a reality in the lives of sinners as the Son lives the pattern after which we are to be remade, and then dies to pay for and defeat our sin (vv. 7-10). The Father sent his Son into the world precisely to accomplish the saving work necessary for those whom he had chosen to be made holy. But even with the plan of the Father and the saving work of the Son, we are not declared holy or remade as holy until we put our faith in Christ. Then, by faith, we begin the life-long process of conformity into his likeness, and here the Spirit directs us to the Son and his work in opening our eyes to see the glory of the Son (2 Cor. 4:6) and in making us like Christ (2 Cor. 3:18). So our sanctification is done by the triune God, with Father, Son, and Holy Spirit each participating in different but complementary ways. How wonderful is the unity and diversity of the trinitarian Persons. Rich harmony is heard from heaven as Father, Son, and Holy Spirit each sing their respective parts of one glorious and intricately unified composition.

6. The triune relationships of the Father, Son, and Holy Spirit cause us to marvel at the *unity* of the triune God.

The three persons are never in conflict of purpose, never jealous over another's position or specific work, never prideful over one's own position or work, and they are always sharing fully the delight in being the one God and accomplishing the unified purpose of God. Here is a unity of differentiation, where love abounds and where neither jealousy nor pride is known. Each divine Person accepts his role, each in proper relation to the others, and each works together with the others for one unified, common purpose. It is nothing short of astonishing to contemplate the fundamental and pervasive unity within the Trinity, given the eternal differentiation that exists in the three Persons.

7. The triune relationships of the Father, Son, and Holy Spirit cause us to marvel at the *diversity* within the triune God.

The three Persons of the Godhead exhibit distinct roles in relation to one another. Distinct tasks and activities in accomplishing their common plan characterize nearly all of the work that the true and living God undertakes. Yet all the while, they carry out this work in complete harmony of activity and unity of purpose. As amazing as the fundamental unity of God is, so too is his fundamental "division of labor." The Father is the eternal Father, the Son the eternal Son, and the Spirit eternally distinct from both Father and Son. This diversity speaks of the richness of God, while never allowing the richness of differentiation to lead to discord. As we rightly marvel at the unity of God, we also rightly marvel at how the eternal relations among the triune Persons constitute an eternal yet harmonious differentiation within the one God.

8. The triune relationships of the Father, Son, and Holy Spirit cause us to wonder at the *social relationality* of the triune God.

God is never "alone." He never experiences, whether with or without the world he has made, a sense of individual isolation and "loneliness." He never has been lonely or alone, in this sense, nor could he ever be, even in principle. The one God is three! He is by very nature both a unity of Being while also existing eternally as a society of Persons. God's tri-Personal reality is intrinsic to his existence as the one God who alone is God. He is a socially related being within himself. In this tri-Personal relationship the three Persons love one another, support one another, assist one another, team with one another, honor one another, communicate with one another, and in everything respect and enjoy one another. They are in need of nothing but each other throughout all eternity. Such is the richness and the fullness and the completion of the social relationship that exists in the Trinity.

9. The triune relationships of the Father, Son, and Holy Spirit cause us to marvel at the *authority-submission structure* that exists eternally in the three Persons in the Godhead, each of whom is equally and fully God.

An authority-submission structure marks the very nature of the eternal Being of the one who is three. In this authority-submission structure, the three Persons understand the rightful place each has. The Father possesses the place of supreme authority, and the Son is the eternal Son of the eternal Father. As such, the Son submits to the Father just as the Father, as eternal Father of the eternal Son, exercises authority over the Son. And the Spirit submits to both the Father and the Son. This hierarchical structure of authority exists in the eternal Godhead even though it is also eternally true that each Person is fully equal to each other in their commonly possessed essence. The implications are both manifold and wondrous as we ponder this authority-submission structure which not only is accepted but is honored, cherished, and upheld within the Godhead.

10. The doctrine of the Trinity—one God existing in three Persons in the ways we have described—provides one of the

most important and neglected *patterns* for how human life and human relationships are to be conducted.

In the end, the doctrine of the Trinity is eminently practical, and the church can benefit much from understanding and modeling its own life, work, and relationships after the Trinity. As we understand better the nature of the Trinity—the unity and diversity in the ways God has revealed himself to us—we have the opportunity to pattern what we do after God's design. We are made in the image of God, and so we can live rightly and best only when we mirror in our relationships the relationships true of the eternal God himself. Yes, we are called to be like God in character, but we also are created to be like God in relationship with one another. To miss this is to miss part of the wonder of human life, and it stems from failing to see something more of the wonder of God himself. May we see in the Trinity, the Father, Son, and Holy Spirit, how their relationships are expressed, and may we learn from this something better about how our relationships and work ought to be lived out, for our good and for the glory of his great and triune name.

2

BEHOLDING THE WONDER OF OUR TRIUNE GOD: HISTORICAL OVERVIEW

INTRODUCTION

God cares that we know who he is, and he longs for us to understand him rightly, according to what he has revealed in his Word. And not only must we seek to know God from Scripture, we should also seek to understand how the doctrine of the Trinity was formulated by early Christians—and how it has endured as generation after generation has reaffirmed this understanding of God. If we fail to understand rightly what the church has held in this crucial doctrine, we run the risk of having misconceptions of God and even of promoting heresy. On the other hand, to understand rightly just how God is both one and three is to enter into some of Scripture's most glorious truths and to share with Christians through the ages the joy of beholding the wonder of our triune God.

In this chapter we will sketch a brief overview of just how early Christians came to understand God as Triune. What is it that we Christians affirm when we sing and recite and pray to the true and living God who is Father, Son, and Holy Spirit? One God, yet a Godhead of three; three Persons, yet one God—how did we arrive

at this understanding? Is it truly the teaching of Scripture, and must
we believe this same truth today? Why did the church insist so early
that we hold this doctrine of God? Does it have any impact upon
our larger theological understanding? Further, does it matter in
terms of our own lives of faith and worship and prayer? Let us consider, then, just why Christian believers have come to affirm this
doctrine.

WHY DID CHRISTIANS COME TO ACCEPT THE DOCTRINE OF THE TRINITY?

Scriptural Monotheism

Just how did the early Christians arrive at the doctrine of the
Trinity?[1] The story here is fascinating, and we owe much to their
hard work, prayers, and struggles to understand what Scripture
requires us to see about God. Most of the earliest Christians, of
course, were converted out of Judaism. Judaism, as you know, is a
monotheistic religion. That is, the Jews believed that there is only
one God, and this God is Yahweh, the God of Abraham, Isaac, and
Jacob. Importantly, the early Christians continued to affirm their
belief in one God. In agreement with their Jewish heritage, the early
church affirmed as strongly as ever that there is only one God, that
the God of the Old Testament was the same God as the God of
Christians, and that both Old and New Testaments taught clearly
that true religion must be monotheistic.

It was remarkable, however, that the early church never seriously considered wavering in its monotheism. The early Christians
lived in the midst of cultures in the Graeco-Roman world that were
dominantly polytheistic. That is, most people in first-century Greek
and Roman societies believed in a multitude of gods. Recall for a
moment the experience of the apostle Paul when he arrived in
Athens. As recorded in Acts 17:16ff., Paul went into Athens expecting friends to join him. And while he waited for them, he walked

up and down the streets of Athens and observed the multitude of altars and shrines and inscriptions, giving evidence that the Athenians worshiped a full pantheon of gods. When later he was asked to speak to them about the God he knew, he began by noting what a religious people the Athenians were, yet that tragically they were worshiping false gods.

In light of the predominance of polytheism throughout the Graeco-Roman world, wouldn't it have been the most natural thing—the easiest thing for Christians to do—simply to adjust their previous monotheistic conviction, and now assert that actually Christians believe in three gods? "You know," they might reason, "we thought there was one God, and that's what we believed from the Old Testament, but now we see that, in fact, there are three Gods—Father, Son and Holy Spirit." But remarkably (and thankfully), this did not happen! Given cultural pressures, given that this would have been the easy way out for the early church, it is noteworthy that the early Christians never seriously entertained this option. Rather, they took the hard way. As we'll see, they continued to affirm, with the Old Testament and with their Jewish heritage, that there was one and only one God, even though the Father is God, the Son is God, and the Holy Spirit is God. Why did they do this? They went the hard route simply because they believed the Bible. Let's rehearse briefly some of the evidence that the early Christians considered which makes it clear that both Old and New Testaments affirm a monotheistic faith.

Old Testament support for monotheism. The Old Testament declares in no uncertain terms that there is one and only one God. In fact, the opening verse of the Bible, rightly understood, declares this truth with boldness and clarity. Genesis 1:1 reads, "In the beginning, God created the heavens and the earth." Whatever else Genesis 1 is about, the main thing it teaches is that there is *one God*. But how does it do that? It does so by affirming that God created all that is, the heavens and the earth; there are no other gods claiming territorial jurisdiction. There is not one god of the sun, one god of the moon, one god of the stars, one god of the mountains. No, there is one God of the stars, the moon, the sun, the mountains, and everything! "In the beginning, God created the heavens and the earth" is a straightforward affirmation of monotheism. As was true for the early church, the Old Testament covenant people of God were surrounded by polytheistic cultures. The Assyrians, the Babylonians, the Phoenicians, the Philistines, and all of the other cultures around Israel affirmed the existence of a variety of gods, each having some territorial authority and rulership. But for the people of Israel, it was not so. From the very first verse of the Bible forward, Old Testament religion declared and celebrated that there is one and only one God. He created everything, and he is Lord of all by virtue of his being Creator of all.

Besides this opening declaration of monotheism, consider some other Old Testament affirmations of monotheism. In Deuteronomy 4:35, Moses says, "To you it was shown, that you might know that the LORD is God; there is no other besides him." Echoing this same thought, Moses again declares in Deuteronomy 6:4, "Hear, O Israel: the LORD our God, the LORD is one." The last phrase can be translated either as "the LORD is one" or "the LORD alone," but in either case it emphasizes that there is but one God. The Lord alone is God.

First Kings 8:59-60 proclaims Israel's monotheistic faith in beautiful terms. Here, in Solomon's address after the temple has been built, he declares, "Let these words of mine, with which I have pleaded before the LORD, be near to the LORD our God day and night, and may he maintain the cause of his servant and the cause of his people Israel, as each day requires, that all the peoples of the earth may know that the LORD is God; there is no other." What a statement! Again, recall the polytheistic environment surrounding Israel when Solomon made this pronouncement. He was declaring that no one else is God—not Baal, not Ashteroth, nor any of the gods of the nations around Israel—only Yahweh is God. There simply is no other God.

In another remarkable passage, the Lord speaks through the prophet Isaiah and says, "I am the LORD, and there is no other, besides me there is no God; I equip you, though you do not know me, that people may know, from the rising of the sun and from the west, that there is none besides me; I am the LORD, and there is no other" (Isa. 45:5-6). God wants to go on record that he is able to do his work—in this case raising up Cyrus, though Cyrus will never know how God is using him—only because he alone is the true and living God. Four times in these two verses, God declares that he has the sole claim on true deity ("there is no other," "besides me there is no God," "there is none besides me," and "I am the LORD and there is no other"). God alone, then, is God, and his declaration of this through Isaiah is unequivocal and absolute.

Finally, reminiscent of the previous passage is Isaiah 46:9, in which God again declares, "Remember the former things of old; for I am God, and there is no other; I am God, and there is none like me." Clearly God wants his people to know that there is only one God, and that he—Yahweh, the covenant God of Israel—is the true and living God.

The early Christians, then, had strong and clear reason from Old Testament revelation to affirm that God is one. But does the New Testament affirm there is one God? Does this teaching carry forward, or is monotheism somehow compromised or rejected when Jesus comes as the eternal Son of the eternal Father? We turn now to some of the most important New Testament teaching affirming monotheism.

New Testament support for monotheism. The New Testament also declares in no uncertain terms that there is one and only one God. For example, John 17:3 asserts, "And this is eternal life, that they know you the only true God." Only God can give eternal life, and the God who does this is one. And 1 Corinthians 8:6 says plainly, "Yet for us there is one God, the Father, from whom are all things and for whom we exist." The truth of this passage is reminiscent of Genesis 1:1, where we first learned that the one God created the heavens and the earth. Only one God is Creator of all, and he likewise is Lord of all he has made. As he owns all that is, he owns us. He has rights over us. We exist for him. There is one God, and to this one God we owe our absolute allegiance.

First Timothy 2:5 likewise declares, "For there is one God, and there is one mediator between God and men, the man Christ Jesus." While this verse would wrongly be interpreted to say that Jesus is *only* a man and therefore is not God, it rightly teaches that that there is but one God. We will consider later just how Jesus relates to the monotheistic teaching of both Old and New Testaments. Here again, though, we see that God is one.

Romans 3:29-30 asserts, "Or is God the God of Jews only? Is he not the God of Gentiles also? Yes, of Gentiles also, since God is one. He will justify the circumcised by faith and the uncircumcised through faith." The God of the Jews and the God of the Gentiles, who brings both together by faith in Christ, is one God. He is not one god for the Jews and a different god for the Gentiles. He is one God—the God both of the circumcised and the uncircumcised, who come together to this one God through faith in Christ.

Finally, James 2:19 declares, "You believe that God is one; you do well. Even the demons believe—and shudder!" How sad it would be if the church were to deny what even the demons get right! Thankfully, this was not the case. Rather, early Christians uniformly affirmed what both Old and New Testaments declare with consistency, clarity, and forcefulness, namely, that there is but one God, and that the covenant God of Israel and the God and Father of our Lord Jesus Christ are one and the same God. The God of both Testaments, then, is the one true and living God.

Scriptural Trinitarianism: Key Biblical Teachings

Now here is where the story becomes even more interesting, because early Christians noticed that there was more taught in the Bible, particularly in the New Testament, than that there is one God. Clearly, both Testaments are monotheistic, but the New Testament especially also taught truths about Jesus and the Holy Spirit that raised questions in the minds of thoughtful early Christians. How are we to understand who Jesus is when there is one God? All agreed that there was really no question but that the Father is God. Whose will did Jesus come to obey, if not the will of God, his Father? And, whom did Jesus seek to glorify if not God the Father who sent him? Therefore, there simply was no serious dispute in the early church over the full and unqualified deity of the Father. But how should we understand Jesus? Yes, he is our Lord, and we honor and worship him as our Savior. But how are we to affirm with Thomas in his confession in John 20:28, what he exclaims regarding the risen Christ, "My Lord and my God!"? If the Father is truly God, and we believe in only one God, what do we say about Jesus?

To add to this fundamental question regarding the true identity of Jesus, the early Christians noticed that even some of the very passages affirming that there is one God raised questions regarding the identity of Jesus in relation to their monotheistic conviction. Look again at John 17:3. I purposely quoted only part of the verse earlier. Consider now the whole verse: "And this is eternal life, that they know you the only true God, and Jesus Christ whom you have sent." Now think carefully about what this is saying. The "and" that couples together "the only true God" and "Jesus Christ whom you have sent" seems to indicate the one true God and Jesus Christ are equivalent. "Who can give eternal life?" one might inquire. And the answer to that question from all of Scripture clearly is, "Only God can give eternal life." Given this, consider again what this verse asserts. Eternal life comes by knowing the only true God *and* Jesus

Christ whom the Father has sent. In other words, because it says eternal life comes from both the Father and Jesus Christ, the passage displays Christ as equivalent to the Father. Only God can give eternal life, yet here both the Father and the Son give eternal life. The one God, it would seem, is both the Father and the Son. But this is not all. The "and" also indicates that the Father and Jesus Christ are distinct. There is no unnecessary redundancy when John writes that eternal life is found in knowing "the only true God and Jesus Christ." Rather, while both give eternal life, so indicating their commonality, yet the two are distinguished, indicating their distinction from each other. So we have in this one verse an indication of the Father's and Son's equivalency and also their difference, of their identity with one another and their distinction from one another. But just how can it be both ways? How can we have both at the same time? These questions loomed large in the early centuries of the church.

Or consider again 1 Corinthians 8:6. In this case as well, we have looked at only the first half of the verse. Here is the whole verse: "Yet for us there is one God, the Father, from whom are all things and for whom we exist, and one Lord, Jesus Christ, through whom are all things and through whom we exist." We have the same kind of tension here as we saw in John 17:3. After all, who is Creator of all that is? Answer: Only God can create the heavens and earth, as Genesis 1:1 makes abundantly clear. But here we have in this one verse an affirmation that the one God, the Father, is Creator of all, *and* (note again the significance of the "and" joining these two concepts) the one Lord Jesus Christ, who likewise is said to create all things. So which is it? Is God the Father Creator? Or is the Son the Creator? The answer according to this verse is this: they both are. So, once again we see that since only God can create, yet both the Father and the Son are said to create, the Father and Son are thereby identified together as the one Creator. Yet since the two are spoken of separately, we must affirm also a proper distinction between the

Father and the Son. The one God is identified as both Father and Son, while Father and Son are distinguished from each other. Identity and distinction, equivalency and difference—this is the reality the early Christians faced as they pondered carefully and seriously what the New Testament taught them about Jesus and his relation to the Father.

Many other New Testament passages raise this same question of the relation of the Son to the Father. For example, John 1:1: "In the beginning was the Word, and the Word was with God [distinction], and the Word was God [identity]." The profundity of this opening verse of John's Gospel is beyond full human comprehension. Notice first that John intentionally begins with echoes of Genesis 1:1 by asserting "In the beginning" and then following immediately in John 1:3 with an affirmation of the Word as Creator: "All things were made through him [i.e., the Word], and without him was not any thing made that was made." So, exactly who was "in the beginning" as Creator of all that is? Answer: the Word! This Word, then, must be understood as God. And this is only confirmed as John declares at the end of John 1:1, "and the Word was God." No question, then, the Word who was in the beginning, who was Creator (clear connections with the God of Genesis 1) is himself God. Both by direct statement and by conceptual linkage with creation, the Word is God.

But this is not all. Amazingly, this Word of John 1:1, who is God, is also said to be "with God." There is a distinction, as well as an identity, between "the Word" and "God." Some difference exists between the Word and God, while the Word simultaneously is God. And in case we wonder just who this Word is, all we need do is read a bit further and we realize this Word is none other than the incarnate Son of the Father, Jesus Christ. For John 1:14 declares, "And the Word became flesh and dwelt among us, and we have seen his glory, glory as of the only Son from the Father, full of grace and truth." So, how can we talk about Jesus in a way that understands him as identical to God ("the Word was God," linked with the Creator God of Genesis 1) while simultaneously being distinguished from God ("the Word was with God")? He has the same identity as God, as the Father, and yet he is different from the Father. He is with God, yet he is God. How can we understand all of this together?

And consider also just a few of Jesus' own claims. One of the most famous and most important here is Jesus' self-affirmation in John 8:58, where he said to the Pharisees, "Truly, truly, I say to you, before Abraham was, I am." Let's not miss the significance of this claim. Jesus is not merely saying that he already existed before Abraham existed. This would be remarkable enough in itself (since Abraham lived roughly 2,000 years before Christ!), but it was not his main point. That is, it is not that Jesus was "merely" claiming to have lived before the time of Abraham. If that's all he was saying, you would think that this poor Nazarene was a crackpot; you'd want to call for the men in white coats to come and pick him up. But clearly the Pharisees did not respond this way to Jesus. No, rather, they responded by picking up stones to throw at him—because they considered that here, again, Jesus had committed blasphemy. They knew his claim was, at its root, a claim of deity.

For you see, in Exodus 3, Moses asked the Lord, When I go back to the people of Israel and they ask me who sent me to you, what shall I say to them? We read in Exodus 3:14, "God said to Moses, 'I AM WHO I AM.' And he said, 'Say this to the people of Israel, "I AM [Yahweh] has sent me to you."'" Jesus, then, is claiming to be none other than Yahweh of the Old Testament, the God whose name eternally is "I am." No wonder the Pharisees concluded that Jesus had uttered blasphemy.

Another very instructive passage is Mark 2. You'll recall that here some friends of a needy paralytic man lowered him through the roof of a house where Jesus was, and Jesus said something fully unexpected. In verse 5 we read, "And when Jesus saw their faith, he said to the paralytic, 'My son, your sins are forgiven.'" Mark then records the response by some who heard Jesus: "Now some of the scribes were sitting there, questioning in their hearts, 'Why does this man speak like that? He is blaspheming! Who can forgive sins but God alone?'" (vv. 6-7). Amazing! Chalk one up for the scribes: they got this one right. "Who can forgive sins but God alone?" Absolutely no one can forgive sins but God, so what, then, must be Jesus' point? To put it simply, Jesus was declaring before all, "I am God." And so as to reinforce the point, in verses 10-11 Jesus says, "'But that you may know that the Son of Man has authority on earth to forgive sins'—he said to the paralytic—'I say to you, rise, pick up your bed, and go home'." The physical miracle attested to the spiritual truth about Jesus. He was, in fact, the Son of Man who was God in human flesh with the authority to forgive sins; therefore, Jesus was God.

Another remarkable chapter upholding the deity of Christ is Hebrews 1. Consider from this single chapter six separate and strong indications that Jesus is God. First, the letter to the Hebrews begins, "Long ago, at many times and in many ways, God spoke to our fathers by the prophets, but in these last days he has spoken to us by his Son, whom he appointed the heir of all things, through whom also he created the world" (Heb. 1:1-2). As in John 1:3, 1 Corinthians 8:6, and (as we shall see) Colossians 1:16, Christ is here specified as the Creator of all that is. Yet because only God can create, Christ clearly must be God.

Second, Hebrews 1:3 continues, "He is the radiance of the glory of God and the exact imprint of his nature." In Isaiah 42:8, God declares in no uncertain terms, "I am the LORD; that is my name; my glory I give to no other, nor my praise to carved idols." And yet, Hebrews declares that Jesus (alone) fully and exactly exhibits the very nature and glory of God. Jesus is the exact representation of his nature. But God is incomparable, and none will share his glory. Therefore, Jesus must be himself God, for only God can possess the nature of God and share the glory of God.

Third, Hebrews 1:3 also affirms that the Son "upholds the universe by the word of his power." Not only is the Son Creator of all (Heb. 1:2), he is also the Sustainer of all (v. 3). Only God possesses the almighty power necessary to uphold and sustain this vast universe, and the Son is here declared to do just this. The Son, then, is God.

Fourth, Hebrews 1:6 states, "And again, when he brings the firstborn into the world, he [God] says, 'Let all God's angels worship him.'" We should be astonished at the significance of this statement for understanding the New Testament's portrayal of Christ. For here, God is envisioned commanding his angels to *worship the Son* who comes into the world. And, of course, we know this actually happened, when with the shepherds, the angels worshiped the Son at the announcement of his birth (Luke 2:13-14). But notice: Who is it in Hebrews 1:6 who commands the angels to worship the Son? *God* does. Yet remarkably, the Old Testament clearly taught that only God is to be worshiped, as Jesus himself declared when tempted by the devil. Jesus cited Deuteronomy 6:13 when he responded to Satan, "You shall worship the Lord your God, and him only shall you serve" (Luke 4:8). Therefore, only God is to be worshiped, as God himself had declared and Jesus himself knew full well. Yet Hebrews 1:6 tells us that when the Son comes into the world, God *commands* the angels to *worship him.* That is, the God who knows and declares that only God is to be worshiped, commands that his Son be worshiped. By God's own declaration, then, Jesus himself can only rightly be understood as God.

Fifth, Hebrews 1:8 records for us, "But of the Son he [God] says, 'Your throne, O God, is forever and ever, the scepter of uprightness is the scepter of your kingdom.'" Whereas in Hebrews 1:6 we see God commanding the Son to be worshiped, commanding an action appropriately directed only toward God, here we have God actually calling Jesus "God." The Greek word *theos,* the most common Greek word for God, is here used by God of Jesus.

And sixth, Hebrews 1:10-12 quotes Psalm 102:25-27, applying this Old Testament text to Jesus. But as one examines the Psalm quoted in its context, it is clear that the psalmist is extolling the greatness, the eternity, the immutability of the true and living God. Unlike all else that changes and comes to an end, the God of Israel, the true and living God, never changes, and his life never comes to an end. But Hebrews 1:10-12 quotes this marvelous text from Psalm 102 and indicates that these truths are about none other than the Son! Jesus, then, is the eternal and immutable (cf. Heb. 13:8) God over all. He, the Son of the Father, is God, while the Father likewise is God. How remarkable and how amazing this is. But how shall we understand these teachings of the New Testament in light of our commitment to monotheism?

My main point in all of this is not, in itself and alone, to demonstrate the deity of Christ. While this is gloriously true, the main purpose has been to demonstrate the tension faced by the early church fathers in endeavoring to understand who Jesus truly is in relation to the Father (God), and in light of the Bible's clear teaching that there is one and only one God. Early Christians continued to believe there is one God, but they came to a growing conviction that not only is the Father God, but Jesus likewise must be understood as God. How could this be, and just "what language shall we borrow" to affirm and explain this teaching of Scripture?

Scriptural Trinitarianism: The Church's Formulation

Of course, some did not think it possible to make sense of both the Father and Jesus being eternally divine, without compromising monotheism. Some, in an endeavor to protect the "monarchy" or exclusive kingly rulership of the Father, sought to explain who Jesus is differently than the final orthodox formulation would later suggest. Two views in particular played an important role in helping the early Christians think more carefully about Jesus in contrast to these views that were seen, ultimately, as heretical.

First, an early Christian by the name of Sabellius proposed that there is only one God, who is the Father, but that the Father decided to manifest himself at one point in human history in the "mode" of the Son, coming into the world as Jesus Christ of Nazareth. So, the one God and Father of all was now manifested as the Son and not the Father, whereas before the incarnation, he had always subsisted in the mode of being the Father. Then, after the resurrection and ascension of Christ, the one God came in the "mode" of the Holy Spirit, so that during this time when the Holy Spirit is present and at work, God subsists as the Holy Spirit and not as the Father or as the Son. This view, called "modalism," proposed then that while the Father is fully God, the Son is fully God, and the Holy Spirit is fully God, nevertheless God manifests himself in only one such "mode" at a time. God, then, is *successively* Father, Son, and Holy Spirit; he is not *simultaneously* Father, Son, and Holy Spirit. No church council was needed to convince Christian people that this view simply could not account for Scripture's teaching. All one need do is consider the baptism of Jesus, or Jesus' prayer in the garden of Gethsemane, to realize that the Bible requires that the Father, Son, and Holy Spirit must each be present and subsisting at the same time. God, then, must be simultaneously Father, Son, and Holy Spirit, not just one of these "modes" of the divine expression at a time.

Second, a bishop by the name of Arius proposed that while Jesus is highly exalted and worthy of being honored, yet Jesus should be seen merely as the first and greatest creation of the one true God, not as God himself. Arius proposed this idea in order to maintain the belief that there is one God and one God only, and not to jeopardize that fundamental conviction. So, argued Arius, although Jesus is far above us, nonetheless, he is a creature who is not himself the eternal God. Unlike the modalistic view of Sabellius, the Arian view gained a large following, and to address it, a church council was called at Nicea in A.D. 325. At the Council of

Nicea, a number of Arians were present arguing the position of their leader. But the hero of the Council of Nicea was a bishop by the name of Athanasius. Athanasius was a very gifted, godly theologian who defended the deity of Christ against Arius's view that Christ was merely a highly exalted created being. No, argued Athanasius, the New Testament record is so clear and strong for Christ's deity that we must affirm that Christ is of the very *same nature* as the Father. The Greek word that Athanasius used here is *homoousios* (from *homo,* "same," and *ousios,* "nature"), indicating that Christ possessed the identically same nature as the Father. Some at Nicea proposed that perhaps if we said that Christ was *homoiousios* (from *homoi,* "similar," and *ousios,* "nature") with the Father, this would be sufficient. But Athanasius prevailed, and the Nicene Creed that was written, and that is still recited in many of our churches today, insisted that Christ was "one nature" or the identically "same nature" (*homoousios*) with the Father.

But what about the Holy Spirit? Did the church also believe the Holy Spirit was God? Yes, the church came to the strong conviction, also, that the Holy Spirit was fully God; but this issue was not taken up directly until after the question of the Son was settled at the Council of Nicea. The big question to solve, obviously, was, What do we say about Jesus? But now, having settled that Jesus is fully God, and that he possesses the identically same nature as the Father, attention turned to how we should understand the Holy Spirit. And, as with the question of the nature and identity of the Son, here also a number of Scriptural passages came to the fore as demonstrating that the Holy Spirit is God. Consider briefly just some of the biblical evidence for the Spirit's deity.

Acts 5:3-4 is a telling passage in this regard. As the account in Acts 5 unfolds, we are told that Ananias and Sapphira had sold property and received the proceeds from this sale, but had brought only a portion of this money to the apostles while claiming to give all of it. By the Spirit's illumination, Peter was able to know that they had lied, and so he said, "Ananias, why has Satan filled your heart to *lie to the Holy Spirit* and to keep back for yourself part of the proceeds of the land? While it remained unsold, did it not remain your own? And after it was sold, was it not at your disposal? Why is it that you have contrived this deed in your heart? You have not *lied* to men but *to God*" (Acts 5:3-4). So to lie to the Holy Spirit is to lie to God. As Peter here indicates, the Holy Spirit truly is God.

Consider also 1 Corinthians 2:10-11. Here Paul says that God has revealed truth to him and to other apostles "through the Spirit." But notice further what he says: "These things God has revealed to us through the Spirit. For the Spirit searches everything, even the depths of God." Even if we were to stop reading at this point, there still would be sufficient reason for concluding that the Holy Spirit is God, because only God can search the depths of God. But the next verse makes this conclusion even stronger. Paul continues, "For who knows a person's thoughts except the spirit of that person, which is in him? So also no one comprehends the thoughts of God except the Spirit of God." Is it not the case that if the Spirit "comprehends the thoughts of God" the Spirit is omniscient? But since only God can fully know the thoughts of God, it follows that the Spirit truly is God.

By analogy, another text speaks powerfully of the Spirit's deity. In 1 Corinthians 3:16, Paul asks, "Do you not know that you are God's temple and that God's Spirit dwells in you?" From an Old Testament perspective, consider the richness of the metaphor Paul uses, this notion of the temple. Who, from the time the temple was built, resided in the temple? Whose glory was manifested in the temple? Clearly, it was the glory of God that descended and was manifested in the temple. Here Paul says that the Spirit of God is now inhabiting the temple, indicating by this that the Spirit of God is God himself. Since God inhabits the temple, and Paul now applies this concept to the Spirit, it follows that the Spirit is God who indwells the temple. Though the temple now changes, amazingly, from an external building to our very bodies and lives, yet the point about the Spirit is clear. Because God inhabits the temple, and because we are now the temples of God whose Spirit indwells our lives, God dwells in us as his Spirit indwells us. Therefore, the Spirit of God is God.

One last passage in support of the Spirit's deity is both brief and clear. Hebrews 9:14 makes reference to the work of Christ on the cross, noting simply that ". . . Christ, who through the eternal Spirit offered himself without blemish to God . . ." accomplished our salvation. So, how did Jesus go to the cross? How did Jesus obey the greatest, hardest, most challenging of all the commandments that the Father gave him to do? Yes, he was "obedient to the point of death, even death on a cross" (Phil. 2:8), but how did he accomplish this greatest of all works? Hebrews answers here with the brief but profound comment that Christ offered himself up *by the eternal Spirit*. The Spirit that worked within him all through his life empowered him to obey the Father and go to the cross. This was God's work in Christ, and it was accomplished in him by the eternal Spirit. The eternal Spirit of Hebrews 9:14, then, can be none other than the Spirit who is himself God.

The church saw these and many other passages supporting the deity of the Spirit; and despite opposition to the Spirit's deity following the Council of Nicea, the church affirmed also the full and equal deity of the Holy Spirit. Another ecumenical council was called, this one at Constantinople in A.D. 381. Here, the heroes were the Cappadocian Fathers, whose names are Basil, Gregory of Nyssa, and Gregory of Nazianzus. These three courageous theologians defended the Spirit's deity, and in the end, the Council of Constantinople expanded the Nicene Creed to affirm that the Holy Spirit, the Lord and Life-Giver, proceeds from the Father and is to be worshiped with the Father and the Son. He too, then, is only rightly understood as fully God.

And yet there is one God! Father, Son, and Holy Spirit each is fully God, but there is one and only one God. This obviously was puzzling to many, yet the early Christians saw in Scripture itself language that suggested exactly this three-in-one relationship of the Godhead. Many so-called "triadic" passages were noted, texts of Scripture where God is spoken of as one, yet all three members of the Godhead are mentioned. Think here of two in particular. First, in Jesus' great commission to his disciples, he instructs them, "Go therefore and make disciples of all nations, baptizing them in the name of the Father and of the Son and of the Holy Spirit" (Matt. 28:19). Notice that believers are to be baptized into the *name* (singular) of God, yet the name of this one true and living God is Father, Son, Spirit. The fact that Jesus uses the singular "name" rather than the plural "names" indicates that God is one and that his nature, signified by his name, is singular, not plural. There is one God, not many. Yet this singular name is itself differentiated among three Persons, so that Father, Son, and Holy Spirit comprise the one God in whose name we are baptized. Yes, God is one, but God is three. Jesus here affirms monotheism, but it is not a unitarian monotheism. Rather, the triadic mention of three Persons of the Godhead shows that only the three together constitute the nature of the true and living God.

Second, Paul concludes his second letter to the Corinthians with this benediction: "The grace of the Lord Jesus Christ and the love of God and the fellowship of the Holy Spirit be with you all" (2 Cor. 13:14). A benediction offers the writer or speaker the opportunity to say, "May God be with you," or "May God richly bless you." But for Paul, the God of the Bible will bless his people as the grace of Christ, the love of the Father ("the love of God"[2]), and the fellowship of the Spirit are present with us. In other words, the one God of New Testament understanding is the God who is Father, Son, and Holy Spirit.

The collective wisdom of the early church fathers culminated finally in the work of Augustine, painstakingly written over nineteen years (from A.D. 400–419), under the title *De Trinitate*, or *Treatise on the Trinity*. In this masterful work, Augustine put together for the church one of the most influential and helpful of all discussions on the doctrine of the Trinity. Essentially, Augustine proposed that we understand the triune nature of God in such a way that we distinguish the senses in which God is one and three, respectively. God is *one in essence* or *nature*, but God is *three in person*. There is no logical contradiction here even if the concept is beyond our complete comprehension. If God were one in essence and three in essence, or if he were one in person and three in person, then we would have a straightforward contradiction. The so-called doctrine of the Trinity, then, would be total nonsense. But this is not the case. Rather, God's "oneness" and "threeness" are in different respects or senses. He is one in essence, so the essence of God is possessed fully by each member of the Trinity. But he is three in person, so the Father is not the Son or the Holy Spirit, although the Father possesses the identically same nature as does the Son and the Holy Spirit.

An orthodox definition of the Trinity, taking from Augustine's and other church fathers' insights, then, would assert the following:

> The doctrine of the Trinity affirms that God's whole and undivided essence belongs equally, eternally, simultaneously, and fully to each of the three distinct Persons of the Godhead.

Now think what this is claiming. It affirms that the Father, Son, and Holy Spirit each possesses the divine nature *equally*, so as to avoid Arianism; *eternally*, so as to avoid thinking of God's nature as created; *simultaneously*, so as to avoid modalism; and *fully*, so as to avoid any tri-partite understanding of the Trinity (e.g., like a pie divided into three equal pieces). The Father, Son, and Holy Spirit are not each one-third God, but each is fully God, equally God, and this is true eternally and simultaneously.

In *essence,* then, each member of the Godhead is identical; but in *person* each is distinct. Much of the doctrine of the Trinity deals with these ideas of both unity and difference, of identity and distinction. In God we find the eternal and singular being of God existing and expressing himself in the three Persons of Father that is not Son or Spirit, Son that is not Father or Spirit, and Spirit that is not Father or Son.

And the three members of the Godhead work together in harmony. Not in unison, but in harmony. "Unison" expresses a form of unity, yet it has no texture and richness. "Harmony," however, communicates the idea of unified expression but only through differing yet complementary parts. You have different voices in different pitches. One carries the melody, but just one. Others carry the strains of harmony to fill out and complement the melody. If you think that only one part matters, you are sorely mistaken. For again, to achieve the kind of textured and rich unity that harmony accomplishes, all the parts are important. Yet each part has to be an expression of the same score, the same composition, expressing the mind of the composer.

So it is with the Trinity: it is God's unified nature expressed richly and beautifully in the three equal and full possessions and manifestations of that one nature, with each "voice" contributing variously, yet with complete unity and identity of nature or essence. The Father, Son, and Holy Spirit are not identical Persons, but they are harmonious in accomplishing the one undivided purpose, one undivided goal, one common work, since they each possess fully the one, undivided divine essence. So, unity and difference, identity and distinction—this marks the triune nature of God most centrally. Just how this identity and distinction gets worked out among the Persons of the Godhead, and what this means to the lives of us who are made in his image—these questions are what will occupy us through the remaining chapters of our study.

3

Beholding the Wonder of the Father

INTRODUCTION

The Christian faith affirms that there is one and only one God, eternally existing and fully expressed in three Persons, the Father, the Son, and the Holy Spirit. Each member of the Godhead is equally God, each is eternally God, and each is fully God—not three gods but three Persons of the one Godhead. Each Person is equal in essence as each possesses fully the identically same, eternal divine nature, yet each is also an eternal and distinct personal expression of the one undivided divine nature.

The Father, then, is fully God. He is not one-third God, but fully God. Yet it is not the Father alone who is fully God, but he eternally exists along with the Son and the Spirit, each of whom also possesses fully the identically same divine nature. Because of this, what distinguishes the Father from Son and Spirit is not the divine nature of the Father. This—the one and undivided divine nature—is also possessed equally and fully by the Son and Spirit. Therefore, what distinguishes the Father is his particular *role* as Father in relation to the Son and Spirit and the *relationships* that he has with each of them. In light of the equality of essence yet the differentiation of role and relationship that the Father has with the Son and Spirit, how may we understand more clearly the distinctiveness of the Father in relation to the Son and Spirit? We turn in this chapter, then, to explore this question, and through this exploration, to marvel more fully at the wonder that is God the Father.

And what a delight it is to contemplate the greatness, the majesty, the fullness, and the richness that is God—the true God, the living God, the Creator of the heavens and the earth, who is also, incredibly, *our* God. It should astonish us to realize that the God whom we here behold is in fact *the* God. He is God over all. He eternally exists in the fullness of his infinite perfections fully apart from all that is. As Creator of all, he likewise is the sovereign ruler of the universe he has made. Yes, God is great, and God is one. And yet this one God is also three. So, for example, when we pray, we address God the Father just as Jesus instructed us. Recall that Jesus said to pray like this: "Our Father in heaven, hallowed be your name. Your kingdom come, your will be done, on earth as it is in heaven" (Matt. 6:9-10). But not only is God the Father seen as exalted and sovereign over all, he also must be seen and sought as our Provider, Protector, Savior, Helper, and Guide. For Jesus instructs us to pray further, "Give us this day our daily bread, and forgive us our debts, as we also have forgiven our debtors. And lead us not into temptation, but deliver us from evil" (vv. 11-13). Yes, the Father over all, who reigns in all the universe is, in fact, the same Father who provides our daily bread, forgives our daily sins, delivers us from daily temptation, and leads us always in the paths of righteousness. He is God the Father, and he is God our Father.

Our focus in this chapter is on God as Father. We will consider primarily his role as the *eternal Father* of the *eternal Son* (i.e., God as Father within the Trinity) as well as his role as the *God and Father of our Lord Jesus Christ* (i.e., God as the Father of the incarnate Son of God). Of course, there are enormous applications and implications as we see more clearly how the Father-Son relationship works, both within the Trinity and within the history of the incarnate Christ.

But before looking at these implications, we'll explore more carefully what it means that God is God the Father, God the Son, and
God the Holy Spirit, united in some senses yet distinct in others.
What is the nature of the role of the Father in relation to his Son and
to the Spirit, and how does their relationship work itself out?

THE FATHER'S UNIQUE ROLE WITHIN
THE TRINITY

What distinguishes the Father as the Father in the Godhead? What
distinguishes the Father from the Son and the Spirit as each possess the same divine nature? Obviously, what is common to them
cannot distinguish the Father from the Son and the Spirit. And
what is common to them is their common divine nature. So we
cannot say, for example, that the Father has the attribute of
omnipotence, and that's what distinguishes him from the Son and
the Spirit. No, the Son and the Spirit each possesses fully the
attribute of omnipotence by possessing fully the undivided divine
nature. Nor could one say that the Father is distinct from the Son
and Spirit in possessing omniscience—that the Father knows
everything that can be known, everything past, present, and future,
but the Son and Spirit lack some portion of this knowledge. This
too would be false, since the Father, Son, and Holy Spirit, as fully
divine members of the Godhead, each possesses the complete and
undivided divine nature, which nature is comprised of all the
attributes that are true of God. Every essential attribute of God's
nature is possessed by the Father, Son, and Spirit equally and fully.
We cannot look at aspects of the *nature of God* as that which distinguishes the Father from the Son or Spirit; rather we have to look
at the *roles and relationships* that characterize the Father uniquely in
relation to the Son and the Spirit. So our question is this: What
characterizes the distinct role and relationship that the Father has
in respect to the Son and the Spirit? In what follows, we will examine four distinguishing aspects of the Father's role and relationship

vis-à-vis the Son and the Spirit, followed by four applications that flow from this understanding.

The Father as Supreme Among the Persons of the Godhead

First, the Father is, in his position and authority, supreme among the Persons of the Godhead. Consider afresh some familiar passages, and think about what they are saying in light of our question of how the Father is distinguished from the Son and Spirit. For example, Psalm 2 begins with the nations raging against God. The peoples are in an uproar. "The kings of the earth set themselves, and the rulers take counsel together, against the LORD and against his anointed" (Ps. 2:2). And, if one wonders how God responds to the nations that are raging against him, it is clear that he is not in the heavens wringing his hands, thinking, "Oh, no, all these people out there are against me. The world is falling apart. What shall I do?" Rather, in verse 4 we read, "He who sits in the heavens laughs; the Lord holds them in derision." Imagine, by way of illustration, how Michael Jordan might respond if a first-grade boy came up to him defiantly and challenged him to a game of one-on-one on the basketball court. It is a weak analogy, by comparison, but God's response indicates how seriously he takes the threatening ragings of the nations. What does God do? God, who sits in the heavens, laughs.

Now, why does God laugh and hold them in derision? He does so because of what he knows he will do to bring judgment against all those who stand against him. For as we read further, "Then he will speak to them in his wrath, and terrify them in his fury, saying, 'As for me, I have set my King on Zion, my holy hill'" (Ps. 2:5-6). Notice that God asserts his rightful jurisdiction over the nations of the world, and he also affirms his authority over the very king whom he sets over the nations. The point is clear. The Father who is above all the nations, is also above the king whom he sets over the nations. The Father's supremacy is both over the nations themselves and over the king whom he places over the nations.

And if we wonder who this king is whom the Father sets over the nations, we see that the king is none other than his own Son. We read of God saying, "I will tell of the decree: The LORD said to me, 'You are my Son; today I have begotten you. Ask of me, and I will make the nations your heritage, and the ends of the earth your possession. You shall break them with a rod of iron and dash them in pieces like a potter's vessel'" (Ps. 2:7-9). As verse 7 is cited in the New Testament books of Acts and Hebrews, the reference here clearly is to the incarnate Son of God, whom the Father places over the nations. God the Father subjects the nations to his rulership by sending God the Son to come as the incarnate Son and King to reign over the world. And as we learn from Revelation 19, the incarnate but now crucified and risen Son, the "Word of God" (Rev. 19:13) and the "King of kings and Lord of lords" (v. 16) will indeed bring forth the wrath of God Almighty on the nations who stand against God. Here, then, is evidence that the Father's role is supreme over that of the Son, for it is the Father who sends the Son, and who puts the Son in his place as king over the nations; and this is fulfilled as the Son of God, who is the Son of David, comes to reign and bring all things into subjection under his feet (Heb. 2:8). Yes, the Father is supreme in the Godhead, as Psalm 2 makes clear.

Consider another passage we've had occasion already to read. In Matthew 6:9-10, Jesus tells us to pray like this: "Our Father in heaven, hallowed be your name. Your kingdom come, your will be done, on earth as it is in heaven." Jesus specifies that prayer is to be made to the Father, and he says this in the very context in which he asserts that the Father is over all. It is (specifically) the *Father's will* that is to be done, and the *Father's kingdom* that is to come. The Father, then, has supremacy over all, as Jesus here acknowledges.

Further, this attitude of bowing to the authority and position of the Father marked Jesus' own life and ministry over and over. Many times Jesus said things such as, "For I have come down from heaven, not to do my own will but the will of him who sent me"

(John 6:38; cf. 4:34; 5:23-24, 30, 36-38; 6:44; 7:28-29; 8:16-18, 42). He commands us to pray for the *Father's kingdom* to come and the *Father's will* to be done. We are to join with Jesus in acknowledging that the Father has supremacy.

Jesus' perspective that the Father is supreme over all is also clearly evident at the end of Matthew 11, where Jesus considers the relation between the Father and those who had heard Jesus preach. Through much of this chapter, Jesus had been preaching and performing miracles with the result that he had been rejected by the religious leaders of Israel, the Pharisees and the teachers of the law. But rather than despairing at this blatant lack of regard by the learned religious authorities, Jesus prayed, "I thank you, Father, Lord of heaven and earth, that you have hidden these things from the wise and understanding and revealed them to little children; yes, Father, for such was your gracious will. All things have been handed over to me by my Father, and no one knows the Son except the Father, and no one knows the Father except the Son and anyone to whom the Son chooses to reveal him" (Matt. 11:25-27). We see here, once again, Jesus' acknowledgment that the Father is the one who reigns over all. He is Lord of heaven and earth, and he reigns sovereignly over what is revealed, when it is revealed, and to whom it is revealed.

This is so much the case that Jesus prays a prayer that most of us, quite honestly, would have a very difficult time praying. But then, perhaps we don't think in the same way Jesus did of God the Father's relation to the belief or unbelief of those who hear the gospel. Look again carefully at just what Jesus prayed first: "I thank you, Father, Lord of heaven and earth, that you have *hidden these things*" from some. For many of us, this language of Jesus simply is not in our vocabulary. We easily and naturally praise God for the second part of what Jesus prayed, when he thanked the Father that he had *"revealed them* to little children." Many of us naturally affirm the second part of the prayer and wince at the first. But both come from the lips of Jesus, and in both ways he demonstrates the Father's supremacy over all. Jesus here acknowledges that the Father is the sovereign Revealer of truth to those whom he chooses and the Withholder of that revelation from others, as he so chooses.

First Corinthians 15:28 is a very important passage on the question of the Father's supremacy over all; it is a text we'll return to in the next chapter when considering the particular role also of the Son. Paul writes, "When all things are subjected to him, then the Son himself will also be subjected to him who put all things in subjection under him, that God may be all in all." This passage can be confusing, simply because of the pronouns used, and we may not be completely sure just who is being spoken of in each part of the verse. Permit me, then, to provide this paraphrase: "At the completion of history, when all things finally and fully are subjected to Jesus Christ the Son, then the Son himself will also be subjected to his own Father, who is the very one who put all things in subjection under his Son, so that God the Father, who is not subjected to anyone—not even to his own Son— may be shown to be supreme and over all that is."

Now, who is the one who subjected all things to the Son? According to Paul, the Father himself is the one who brought it about that absolutely everything in all of creation would be subjected to his Son. But in so doing, the Father is not himself also subjected to the Son. Rather, the Father, by virtue of being the one who brings about the subjection of all things to the Son, is not himself part of what is subjected to Christ. The Father stands above the Son, and the Son gladly acknowledges this fact. In the end, not only will all created things be subjected to Christ, but Christ will then place himself in subjection to his own Father, so that God the Father may be manifested to all of creation as supreme and over all.

Another similar passage is Philippians 2:9-11. Verses 5-8 tell of Christ emptying himself and taking on the role of a humble servant, in order to become "obedient to the point of death, even death on a cross." But then verses 9-11 foretell the outcome of Christ's humiliation through his ultimate and glorious exaltation. Paul writes, "Therefore God has highly exalted him and bestowed on him the name that is above every name, so that at the name of Jesus every knee should bow, in heaven and on earth and under the earth, and every tongue confess that Jesus Christ is Lord, to the glory of God the Father."

Notice three features of this text. First, it is God the Father who highly exalted the Son and bestowed on him his name that is above all other names (Phil. 2:9). Clearly, if the Father is the one who exalts the Son, and if the Father gives to the Son his all-surpassing name, then the Father has supremacy over the Son. The only one who stands above the Son—who himself stands over all of creation—is the Father. Second, the stress on the comprehensive and all-inclusive nature of the subjection of all things to the Son could not be made more clear, or more glorious! Every single knee, in heaven and earth and under the earth, and every single tongue, will confess that Jesus Christ is Lord! What a day this will be, and what deserved glory will come to the Son on this occasion. Absolutely every created being will acknowledge Christ as Lord, including all human and demonic forces who now despise his name. Yes, everything in all of creation will bow before this Son, the Lord of all. But notice, third, perhaps the single most important feature of this passage, for our present discussion. This glorious statement of the exaltation of Christ does not end with every knee bowing and every tongue confessing that Jesus Christ is Lord. Rather, this action is penultimate while the ultimate glory is extended to God the Father (v. 11b). God the Father receives the ultimate and supreme glory, for the Father sent the Son to accomplish redemption in his humiliation, and the Father exalted the Son to his place over all creation; in all these things, the Father alone stands supreme over all—including supreme over his very Son. All praise of the Son ultimately and rightly redounds to the glory of the Father. It is the Father, then, who is supreme in the Godhead—in the triune relationships of Father, Son, and Holy Spirit—and supreme over all of the very creation over which the Son reigns as its Lord.

Finally, one may recall that in Ephesians 1:3 Paul does not say (merely) that God should be praised for every spiritual blessing he has brought to us. He could have said that, surely; it would not have been incorrect. But interestingly, Paul chooses to be more specific, and to frame this glorious text in clear trinitarian terms; he writes, "Blessed be the God and Father of our Lord Jesus Christ, who has blessed us in Christ with every spiritual blessing in the heavenly places" (Eph. 1:3). The Father gets top billing, as it were. All the blessings that we receive come to us from the Father, through the work of his Son, as mediated to us by the Spirit. The Father is supreme over all, and in particular, he is supreme within the Godhead as the highest in authority and the one deserving of ultimate praise. Here, as in these several other texts, Scripture indicates the supremacy of the Father within the very Godhead itself.

The Father as the Grand Architect, the Wise Designer,
of Creation, Redemption, and Consummation

Secondly, the Father is the Grand Architect, the Wise Designer of all that has occurred in the created order. From initial creation through ultimate consummation and everything that happens in between, it is God the Father who is the Architect, the Designer, the one who stands behind all that occurs as the one who plans and implements what he has chosen to do.

One of the strongest and clearest passages demonstrating the Father as Grand Architect over all that occurs is Ephesians 1:9-12. As Paul enumerates the blessings we have from the Father, he says in verse 9 that God has made "known to us the mystery of his will, according to his purpose, which he set forth in Christ." He purposed that Christ would be the focal person, the one at center stage, who brings all of his plan to fruition. It is in his Son that this happens, to be sure. But who designed it? Who willed it to be? Who purposed the "mystery" by which all would be summed up in the Son? The answer, of course, is that it was the Father who designed the plan of this unfolding mystery. And in his grace, he has now made "known to us the mystery of his will, according to his purpose, which he set forth in Christ as a plan for the fullness of time, to unite all things in him [Christ], things in heaven and things on earth" (Eph. 1:9-10). And Paul continues, making even clearer that the Father designed and reigns over all that occurs, ensuring that his plan is fulfilled. Paul writes, "In him [Christ] we have obtained an inheritance, having been predestined according to the purpose of him [the Father] who works all things according to the counsel of his will" (v. 11). What a remarkable statement this is. The Father plans all that occurs, and this plan involves all things being summed up in his very Son. And then the Father works all things according to the counsel of his own will, ensuring that all he has designed will occur. He plans all that occurs to be summed up in his Son (vv. 9-10), then he carries out all things just as he planned them to be (v. 11).

Some have wondered whether the Father actually plans and accomplishes absolutely everything. That is, is it clear from this text that the Father's plan and accomplishment in fact are comprehensive? Indeed this is clear. Consider the use of "all things" in verses 10 and 11. Verse 10 speaks of the Father's instituting a plan for the fullness of time, to unite *all things* in him (Christ), *things in heaven and things on earth*. The use of "heaven" and "earth" makes absolutely certain that Paul intends us to see that the purpose and plan of God is comprehensive. Nothing is left out, and all is united under his Son. So, too, is the fulfillment of this plan comprehensive. According to verse 11, we have obtained an inheritance, having been predestined according to his purpose "who works *all things* according to the counsel of his will." The repetition here of "all things" surely demonstrates that just as God planned comprehensively "all things," so he accomplishes comprehensively "all things," as the supreme Architect

and Designer of all that is. Everything in heaven and earth, everything from initial creation to ultimate eternal life in heaven and hell
is both planned according to the purpose of God's will and accomplished according to the counsel of that very will. Indeed, God is the
Grand Architect, the Wise Designer of everything that happens.

Similarly, yet not as explicit as in Ephesians 1:9-11, Paul comments in Colossians 1:12 that he is "giving thanks to the Father" for
all that God brings to us in his Son. As the passage unfolds, the
Father is shown to be the one who delivers us from the domain of
darkness and has transferred us into the kingdom of his beloved Son
(v. 13). The Father is the one who redeems us in his Son and brings
us forgiveness of sin (v. 14). And it is the Father's work through the
Son—the Son who is his very image (v. 15) and who possesses his
fullness (v. 19)—that accomplishes both the creation (v. 16) and the
reconciliation (v. 20) of the world. So Paul gives thanks to the Father
in verse 12 for everything that occurs, from creation through consummation; and the Father accomplishes it all through his Son. The
Father, then, is the one who has designed and willed and purposed
everything in all of creation. The Father is the Grand Architect, the
Wise Designer of everything that occurs in the created order.

The Father Is the Giver of Every Good and Perfect Gift

Not only is the Father supreme over all in the Godhead, and not
only is he the Wise Designer and Grand Architect; third, the Father
is the Giver of every good and perfect gift. James 1:13 instructs us
that we should never think, when tempted, that we are being
tempted by God, for God does not tempt anyone. Further, God
himself is not tempted. Rather than thinking that God would ever
tempt us, we need to recall, according to James, that "every good gift
and every perfect gift is from above, coming down from the Father
of lights with whom there is no variation or shadow due to change"
(v. 17). Imagine the breadth and significance of this claim. Where
does every single good gift originate? From the Father. Even the gift

of the Son who provides our salvation? Yes, he is a gift from the Father (John 3:16; 1 John 4:10). And the gift of the Spirit who works in our hearts to transform us, to gift us, to minister in the body of Christ? Yes, he too is from the Father (Acts 1:4; 2:33). Every good gift, in all of life, comes ultimately from the Father.

Another great passage that articulates this is Romans 8:31-32. "What then shall we say to these things?" asks Paul. "If God is for us, who can be against us? He who did not spare his own Son but gave him up for us all, how will he not also with him graciously give us all things?" All things. Every good thing. This simply expands upon the promises made by God throughout the Bible. Recall, for example, in Psalm 34 where the young lions "suffer want and hunger; but those who seek the LORD lack no good thing" (Ps. 34:10). With even greater force here in Romans 8, Paul indicates that since the Father has given us his own Son, absolutely nothing else good for us will be withheld.

By analogy, suppose a very wealthy relative of yours, let's say a wealthy uncle, decided to build a mansion for you, sparing no expense. Your new home—the gracious gift of your uncle—was exquisite; it was an absolutely beautiful home, spacious, with state-of-the-art appliances and the finest of furnishings. But after everything was done, you sat down for your first meal in the beautifully decorated dining room and noticed that there wasn't a salt and pepper shaker. If you mentioned to your uncle that you'd appreciate it if a salt and pepper set could be added to the dining room, do you think that your uncle would begrudge you these items? Do you think the uncle who loved you so much to build you this home and furnish it so lavishly would withhold from you a salt and pepper shaker? In infinitely greater fashion, "he who did not spare his own Son but gave him up for us all, how will he not also with him graciously give us all things?" In light of this, to whom do we owe our heart-filled thanksgiving? To our Father. To the Father who sent the Son and provided this for us. He is the giver of every good and perfect gift. What confidence there is in this. What hope there is to realize the God and Father of our Lord Jesus Christ, God *our* Father, is "for us" (v. 31) to such an extent that he has given us his one and only Son. And the one who has given us his Son will not fail to give to us everything that is good for us. To the Father, then, we owe our deepest thanks and highest allegiance.

The Father Often Provides and Works Through the Son and Spirit

Fourth, though the Father is supreme, he often provides and works through his Son and Spirit to accomplish his work and fulfill his will. I am amazed when I consider here the humility of the Father. For, though the Father is supreme, though he has in the trinitarian order the place of highest authority, the place of highest honor, yet he chooses to do his work in many cases through the Son and through the Spirit rather than unilaterally. Rather than saying to the Son and Holy Spirit, "Just stand aside and watch me as I do all the work," it is as if the Father, instead, says to us, "I want you to see my work accomplished through my Son. Look at my Son! Notice my Son! Look at the marvelous obedience he has given to me. Look at the greatness of his grace extended to those who misunderstand and mistreat him. Look at his wisdom and power manifest in creation and in redemption. Look at my Son, for with him I am well-pleased."

In Ephesians 1, after beginning with, "Blessed be the God and Father of our Lord Jesus Christ who has blessed us in Christ with every spiritual blessing" (Eph. 1:3), Paul goes on to show us that every one of those blessings—every single one of them—comes to us in Christ (vv. 4-12). The Father has chosen us *in Christ.* We are predestined to adoption *through Christ.* We are redeemed and forgiven by the *blood of Christ.* The mystery of his will is fulfilled as all things are *summed up in Christ.* Our inheritance is secured by our *predestination in Christ.* And the promised Holy Spirit seals us forever *in*

Christ. So, while we bless the "God and Father of our Lord Jesus Christ" for every spiritual blessing, we also marvel that the Father has designed that every one of these blessings, without exception, comes to us in and only in his Son. How kind of the Father to shine the spotlight on his Son, to the praise of the glory of his grace.

Recall also John 1:14, which says that ". . . we have seen his glory, glory as of the only Son from the Father, full of grace and truth." Again here, rather than the Father insisting that we behold the glory of the Father himself, he shares his glory with his Son. The Son, we are told, radiates with the glory of his Father, and so while we see the Father's character portrayed in the Son, the Father designs for us to see such glory only in his Son. Again, it is as if he says, "Look at my Son. He's just like me. When you see my Son, you see what I am like" (cf. John 14:8-11).

We should notice, however, how little is made of the Spirit. We'll consider this much more in later chapters, but just now it should register in our minds how frequently the Father shines the spotlight on the Son, and yet how much in the background the Spirit is. I find it amazing how little is made of the Spirit. And it's not as if the Spirit is out there saying, "Hey! Don't forget me! I'm here, too. Don't just marvel at the Son; notice me, too!" Far from this, the Spirit himself seeks not to be front and center stage. He is backstage, behind the curtain, and does not want front billing. He does not want to be publicly noticed. So what does he want to do? Astonishingly, he also is saying, as it were, "Look at the Son! Look at Jesus! Consider his grace and greatness, his mercy and his majesty. Consider and follow the Lord Jesus Christ." That the Spirit seeks to glorify the Son is an amazing thing, and something we'll return to in greater detail.

So, while the Father is supreme in the Trinity, while it is his plan and purpose that is accomplished through the Son and Spirit, yet the Father chooses not to work in such a way that the Son and Spirit are sidelined. In fact the Father refuses even to be noticed first and foremost, in order that the central attention might be given to his Son. Despite his supreme authority, he chooses to work so that another, not himself, most fully manifests his (the Father's) own glory. A profound divine humility is demonstrated by the Father in not taking the pride-of-place position. Indeed the Father often does what he does through both the Son and the Spirit, though it is particularly through his one and only Son. It is not as though the Father is unable to work unilaterally, but rather, he chooses to involve the Son and the Spirit.

In many ways, what we see here of the Father choosing not to work unilaterally but to accomplish his work through the Son, or through the Spirit, extends into his relationship to us. Does God need us to do his work? Does God need us to help others grow in Christ? Does God need us to proclaim the gospel so that others hear the good news and are saved? The answer is an emphatic no. He doesn't need any of us to do any of this. Being the omnipotent and sovereign Ruler over all, he would merely have to speak, and whatever he willed would be done. Recall the words of Paul in Acts 17:25, that God is not "served by human hands, as though he needed anything." No, the humbling fact is that God doesn't need any of those whom he calls into his service. So why does he do it this way? Why does he call us into his service, and even command us to "serve the LORD" (Ps. 100:2)? The startling answer is this: He calls us into a service that he doesn't need because he wants so very much to share with us. He's generous. He loves and delights in giving a portion of his glorious work to others and empowering them to do it. Recall that it is *his* work. He could just do it, but it is as if he says, "No, I want you to participate in the privilege and pleasure of my work; I want you to be a part of what I am doing, to share in what I am accomplishing—a work that I do through you, a work I could do myself without you, but a work you'll share in for all eternity."

Here's another delightful example of God's desire to share his work with us. My wife and I have two precious daughters. God has given us the privilege of being the biological parents of these children. As a theologian, I've been led to think somewhat differently about this than perhaps some have. God made the original pair. Adam was formed from the dust of the ground when God shaped him and then breathed into him the breath of life. Then God said it was not good for man to be alone, and so God took a rib from the man and fashioned from this the woman, whom he then brought to the man—a helper suitable for him, specially crafted by God. But then, after the creation of male and female in the image of God (Gen. 1:26-27), God tells them, "Be fruitful and multiply and fill the earth" (Gen. 1:28). In other words, God has now given them the privilege and responsibility of bringing into existence all subsequent image-of-God persons. It is as if God said, "I created the first and original pair of human beings in my very image, and I could continue creating them unilaterally so that you would have no part to play. But instead, you are now to bring about human beings; you are to be fruitful and multiply and fill the earth with my greatest of all creations, humans made in my very image." I believe that this is one of the main reasons why God has made the sexual experience in human life to be as pleasurable and wondrous as it is. Image-of-God procreation is designed to reveal the pleasure God has in creating people in his own image, and the joy of bringing yet more of these humans into existence. We have the privilege of creating image-of-God persons. God didn't have to do it this way. He could have done it himself. But, the Father desires to share. He chooses to give to us some of the most wondrous aspects of his work.

The Father does his work through the Son and through the Spirit, and that generosity in sharing his work with others spills over into how he relates to us. What we see happening at the human level in relationship with the Father happens first in the Trinity. The Trinity is the paradigm, the prototype of what it means for the one who is on top to care deeply and sacrificially about those under his authority. The Father chooses willingly to share the joy of his work with others.

APPLICATION OF THE ROLE OF THE FATHER IN RELATION TO HIS SON AND SPIRIT

The Father, then, is supreme among the Persons of the Godhead. He is the Grand Architect and Wise Designer of everything in the created order. He is the giver of every good and perfect gift. Yet though the Father is supreme, he does much of his work through the Son and the Spirit. How do these understandings of the Father relate to our lives and relationships? Consider four applications from these glorious truths regarding the Father's particular role within the Trinity.

1. Marvel at the wisdom, the goodness, the care, and the thoroughness with which the Father exercises his authority.

The Father is always infinitely wise and good in how he exercises his authority. And he is always meticulously careful and thorough in all that he does. He can rightly be trusted and worshiped. He is worthy of our highest esteem because he exhibits such remarkable wisdom, care, goodness, and thoroughness in how he does his work. We should marvel at this and see in the Father a pattern for human relationships and responsibilities. We'll never succeed in being like him as we should be, but we should see in him the pattern of what any of us who is in a position of authority ought to be like. To exercise authority with wisdom, goodness, care, and thoroughness, and not in self-serving ways, is to be like our heavenly Father.

Who is in a position of authority, with responsibility to pattern his manner of leadership after the Father? Clearly, every married man is in this category. Husbands have rightful authority in their homes with their wives, and if God has blessed them with children, their authority extends also to these precious gifts from the Lord. Husbands should exercise their authority with wisdom, goodness, carefulness, and thoroughness in order to seek the well-being of those under their charge. Husbands should seek to be like their heavenly Father in increasing measure.

Others with this responsibility, such as elders in a local church, mothers (as well as fathers) with their children, or employers in the workplace, or in any arena of life where people are placed under another's authority—these are all spheres where we can look to the Father for the model of how to lead, or how to exercise rightful authority. Surely, none of us can be like the Father in this respect, at this moment, perfectly. But this should not stop us from keeping in view the goal to which we aspire. We should never turn our failure into an excuse not to see the vision of what we ought to be. May this vision of God the Father inspire us and move us to depend on God's strength to lead others in a manner that matches more closely how God leads within the Trinity and in human relationships.

2. Learn from God, the Father, what true fatherhood really is like.

Consider just a few applications from understanding the concept of "father" from God the Father. First, those of us who are fathers can learn what it means to be fathers to our children by observing how God the Father "fathers" us. Though there is much more here than we can discuss fully, here is a sketch of what Scripture indicates in regard to God's fathering of us, his children. On the one hand, God as Father *insists on our respect and obedience.* Recall the Lord's Prayer, which addresses God this way: "Our Father in heaven, hallowed be your name" (Matt. 6:9). God, who is Father, wants his children to approach him with respect and honor. Yes, this is because he is God, but such respect and honor also attaches to his being named "our Father." We see this elsewhere in Scripture. For example, God says to the disobedient religious leaders and rebellious children of Israel, "A son honors his father, and a servant his master. If then I am a father, where is my honor? And if I am a master, where is my fear? says the LORD of hosts" (Mal. 1:6). God as Father requires of his people that they respect him, that they honor him, that they obey him. If we are to father our children as God fathers us, we should cultivate in our homes a healthy atmosphere of respect for our authority, and a proper sense of "fear" before us as their fathers. We do our children no service by allowing them to speak and act in disrespectful ways. Our permissiveness in allowing them to be both disrespectful and disobedient to us only cultivates the same sense of disrespect and disregard toward God, the Father in heaven. The permissiveness and leniency pervasive in even Christian homes today provide a breeding ground for training our children to think that they can do what they please and disregard proper authority. But when they learn instead that their fathers mean what they say, and that they expect the respect and obedience of which they are rightfully deserving, then children grow in an atmosphere where proper authority is followed, including—most importantly—the absolute authority of God. So, on the one hand, God fathers us by calling for our respect and by expecting our obedience.

On the other hand, God fathers us by being *lavish, generous, even extravagant in his care, love, provision, and protection for his children.* "He who did not spare his own Son but gave him up for us all, how will he not also with him graciously give us all things?" (Rom. 8:32). Lavish, generous, extravagant care for his children—this also marks the true heart and action of God, our Father. In light of this, every dad should ask himself, "Do my children *know* how much I love them? Do they sense deep in their souls, both from words I have spoken to them and also from the time and attention I give them, that I love them? Do they know that, along with my insistence on their respect and obedience, my heart also longs deeply for them to have the very best that I can give them as their dad?" Fathers can learn much about being human fathers simply by paying close attention to how God, our heavenly Father, fathers us. We can learn what true fatherhood is, then, by looking at *the* Father over all.

Second, some who have been affected by abuse can learn afresh from our heavenly Father just what true fatherhood is. I have sometimes heard that those who grew up with abusive fathers simply need to remove from their minds the notion of God as Father. This name for God is a barrier to their relationship with him, some have said. But surely this is the wrong solution for a very real problem. Rather than removing "father" from our Christian vocabulary, and in particular from our naming of God, should we not work at having our minds and hearts refashioned so that our very conception of "father" is remade by knowing the true Father over all? That is, instead of encouraging a distancing from God as Father, with love and sensitivity we should say to those who cringe at memories of their fathers, "I've got wonderful news for you. There is a true Father who is drastically different in so many, many ways from the father you had. Meet, will you, the true God and Father of our Lord Jesus Christ. Learn from him just what 'father' really means, and enter into the fullness of his fatherly love, care, wisdom, provision, protection, and security." In other words, let's relearn the paradigm of what "father" is from the Father in heaven. While this may involve a very long and difficult process, it is the only way to make true and genuine progress spiritually, since God has named himself as our Father, and this name is meant to convey rich and glorious spiritual benefit to us, his children. If some wicked and negligent human fathers robbed their children from being able to think of "father" positively and rightly, surely we should not add to this problem now by removing from them any hope of having the concept of "father" restored. This would be to rob them yet once again! No, the pathway to recovery here, the only hope for genuine healing, will be through a deep and prolonged study of who God is, and through learning that this great and gracious God is none other than God our Father.

Third, there exists today a widespread movement to remove from Christian vocabulary, hymnody, and even from the Bible itself, references to God as Father. Motivated by misguided and radical feminist convictions that reject all male headship and see fatherhood language about God as promoting the domination of the male, some would seek to change the very language of God's own self-revelation in order to further their social agenda. But the fact is that we as Christians are not at liberty to modify how God has revealed himself to us. He has chosen specifically masculine language, and this includes terms such as "king," "lord," and "father." Do we claim to know better than God how God himself should be named? It seems clear that what stands behind this movement, at bottom, is really a fundamental dislike of the very notion of authority, and in particular of male authority in settings of the home and the believing community. Sinful resistance to authority in general and to the authority of husbands and elders (both male) in particular leads to a desire to undermine the language used of God as Father. We in the evangelical church need to reaffirm and celebrate the fact that God is our Father. Rather than chafing at this language, it should inspire in us deep and profound thanksgiving, confidence, faith, and hope. It should not surprise us that something cherished in the Christian faith is despised by the world, and we should not be swept along by a movement that turns us away from Scripture's clear teaching and from God's own self-revelation of who he is and what he wants to be called. Yes, naming God as Father helps us see just how radical it is to be a Christian in today's culture. May God grant us grace and strength to be faithful to him by giving him our most sincere respect, obedience, love, and devotion, for he is none other than "our Father."

3. Marvel at how the Father delegates his work to others.

One of the most astonishing features of the Father's distinctive work is his willingness and desire to accomplish his work through others. First and foremost, the Father works through his Son to bring to us, his children, "every spiritual blessing in the heavenly places" (Eph. 1:3). Isn't it amazing that the Father has so designed that no gift that he has for us, no blessing from the storehouse of his treasure, comes to us "directly," as it were? Rather, all of these blessings, for time and eternity, are granted us only in his Son. But the privilege of joining him in his work doesn't stop there. As we will consider more fully in chapter 5, his work is done in many significant ways by the Spirit, who acts as the agent of the Son and the Father. And the Father's work is done even through his human creations, whom he calls and empowers to accomplish his will.

I don't know about you, but I find it amazing just how eager to share the Father is in this regard. I tend toward being something of a perfectionist, and so I like things done *my* way—which too often translates in my mind to the *right* way. I find it difficult to apply this principle and not only to *let* someone else in on the work that I'm doing but even to invite them, knowing that another person now has a hand in doing what I care so much about. But when this sort of participation in the work takes place, clearly the greater value that is served is that of a share not only in the work but in the satisfaction and accomplishment. When others participate, it becomes "our work" even if all was designed and "empowered" by one person. And this principle is most astonishing when seen as carried out by none other than God the Father—the one who can do anything he wants, by himself and without any assistance, but who instead determines to do so much of his work through another. And not only does he work through another; let's take it one step further. When the Father does this work through his Son, he revels in the glory and honor that all of creation pays to the Son for the work he's done. The Father shares his work, and with the Son, he shares his glory (e.g., John 17:5). It is as if the Father says, "Shine the spotlight on my Son, and praise and honor his name." How many of us in positions of authority have a heart to put the spotlight on our subordinates and say, for example, "Look at the work of our youth minister! Look at the work of our music minister, or Sunday school teacher, or seniors' pastor, or lay volunteer! See how wonderfully they share in the ministry of this body of believers. Look at them, and recognize their wonderful contribution among us!" How many of us have a heart to do this? As we look at how the Father operates, we are given reason to marvel at just how sharing he is. He delegates a portion of his meaningful work to others, and he rejoices over their participation. Surely this is a model of how we can and should understand the "work of ministry" in the body of Christ, particularly from the vantage point of those granted positions of authority over others. May God grant us hearts, like our Father's, that seek ways to share the "best" of the work so that others may have the joy of such a rich participation in things that truly matter.

4. Marvel at the Father's retention of ultimate supremacy and highest glory even as he shares his work, and his glory, with the Son and with others.

The Father is supreme in the Trinity, and supreme over all creation, as is seen over and over throughout Scripture. Just recall that even when every knee bows and every tongue confesses that Jesus Christ is Lord, they do so "to the glory of God the Father" (Phil. 2:11). And when the Son has subjected all things to himself, he likewise subjects himself to the Father, "that God [the Father] may be all in all" (1 Cor. 15:28). Therefore, there is a biblical insistence on seeing the Father in his rightful place as supreme among the Persons of the Trinity and supreme over all creation. Rightful positions of authority are respected in Scripture, and the greatest example of this is God the Father.

So while the Father places the spotlight on another, most importantly on his Son, this does not result in the Father saying, "Because my Son has done this, please don't look at me. Don't notice me. Just acknowledge my Son and forget about me, his Father." Rather, the Father retains the place of ultimate and supreme authority over all, and he retains the position for which highest honor and glory is owed. Although the Father is astonishingly sharing and humble in calling others to participate in his work, he will nonetheless be acknowledged and honored as God. When men see the good works that the Father calls us and empowers us to do, they will only rightly "give glory to your Father who is in heaven," says Jesus (Matt. 5:16).

This means, then, that there is a corresponding and counterbalancing truth to the one just articulated above. While the Father shines the spotlight on the Son, surely also the Son longs with every breath and in every deed to give honor and glory to his Father. Jesus was as clear about this as he was about anything. He came only to do the will of his Father, and in all he said and did, he acted only as the Father taught him. As he said in the final days of his earthly life, "I glorified you on earth, having accomplished the work that you gave me to do" (John 17:4). And in this prayer to the Father, Jesus continued with such statements as, "I have manifested your name to the people" (v. 6), "I have given them the words that you gave me" (v. 8), "I have given them your word" (v. 14), "the glory that you have given me I have given to them" (v. 22), and "I made known to them your name, and I will continue to make it known" (v. 26). While Jesus was put in the spotlight by the Father, Jesus never, never failed to understand and to acknowledge that he stood only under his Father. The work he accomplished and the word he spoke were not his own, but they were granted him from the Father. Therefore, the Son sought in all that he said and did to give ultimate and highest glory to his Father.

The application here should be obvious. The youth minister, the music minister, the Sunday school teacher, the seniors' pastor, the lay volunteer who are put in the spotlight by another in authority over them, should, like Jesus, reflect back their honor on the one(s) who have granted them the privilege and the training for their particular ministry. After all, it is not their work, first and foremost; all of us, in any and every capacity, work under another—even if that "other" is Christ, who is Lord of his church. And just as Christ who has the spotlight put upon him acknowledges gladly that he is doing the will of his Father and is seeking to honor his Father in all he says and does, so we too should give due honor and recognition to those in authority over us and not pretend that the work done is ours, independent of them. There is, then, a reciprocal relationship in which the Father focuses attention on the Son, and the Son gives credit and recognition to the Father who rightly deserves ultimate honor and glory.

The lessons here are manifold—in our relationships with one another in ministry, in the workplace, in our homes, between husbands and wives, parents and children, pastors or elders and their staff and congregation. While *those in authority* need to be more like the Father, who lavishes favor on others by calling them to participate in his work, often putting the spotlight on them for their labors of love, *those under authority* need to be more like the Son, who gratefully and obediently embraces the work given him by his Father, and gives highest honor to the Father for all that is accomplished. What a revolution would take place in our homes and churches if such reciprocal honoring of one another took place, all the while maintaining clearly the lines of authority that exist, by God's good purpose and wise design. What lessons we learn, then, from seeing more clearly the distinct role of the Father among the Persons of the triune Godhead.

4

Beholding the Wonder of the Son

INTRODUCTION

There is one and only one God, eternally existing and fully
expressed in three Persons, the Father, the Son, and the Holy Spirit.
Each member of the Godhead is equally God, each is eternally
God, and each is fully God—not three gods but three Persons of
the one Godhead. Each Person is equal in essence as each possesses
fully the identically same, eternal divine nature, yet each is also an
eternal and distinct personal expression of the one undivided
divine nature.

The Son, then, is fully God. He is not one-third God, but fully
God. Yet, it is not the Son alone who is fully God, but he eternally
exists along with the Father and the Spirit, each of whom also possesses fully the identically same divine nature. Because of this, what
distinguishes the Son from the Father and the Spirit is not the
divine nature of the Son. This—the one and undivided divine
nature—is also possessed equally and fully by the Father and the
Spirit. Therefore, what distinguishes the Son is his particular *role*
as Son in relation to the Father and to the Spirit and the *relationships*
that he has with each of them. In light of both the equality of
essence yet the differentiation of role and relationship that the Son

has with the Father and the Spirit, how, then, may we understand more clearly the distinctiveness of the Son in relation to the Father and the Spirit? We turn in this chapter to explore this question, and through this exploration, to marvel more fully at the wonder that is God the Son.

What a great Savior and Lord we have in Jesus who is the Christ. He is the matchless King of kings and Lord of lords, the one who has died for sin, has been raised, has ascended, and who now sits in triumph at the right hand of the Father. Notice that his place is at the *right hand* of the Father, but from that position he reigns over heaven and earth (Eph. 1:20-23). As we shall see throughout this chapter, he is now in the process of bringing everything into subjection under his own feet. There is nothing spinning out of control, despite how our newspapers seem to read some mornings. The King of kings raises up presidents, prime ministers, dictators, and despots, and he puts them down as he wills. The one whose name is above every name, who has conquered Satan, sin, and death, now reigns from his heavenly seat at the right hand of his Father, and his kingdom shall have no end!

Further, amazingly, the Son's main purpose in this era, in this time of history, is to build his church. In fact, Christ reigns over the nations in order to accomplish his purpose of building his church (Matt. 16:18). Paul seems to indicate as much when he writes that the Father has "put all things under his feet and gave him as head over all things to the church" (Eph. 1:22). The headlines of our newspapers announce what has happened in human affairs and in the politics of the nations of this earth. But if there were a heavenly daily newspaper, it would lead with headlines about the growth and expansion of the church, and the subtext of merely secondary developments would concern what happened in national and international politics. That is, the main story from heaven's vantage point is how the Son is building his church, and his rulership of the nations simply functions to fulfill that greater and grander goal.

Yes, we have a great Savior and Lord, and we want to honor him as we study who the Son is in relation to the Father and the Spirit. And as we do so we'll marvel at how Jesus Christ embodies most fully both what it is to be God and what it is to be man. In both respects we will behold the glory of who Jesus is. But our perspective on Jesus will come as we consider him in relation both to the Father and to the Spirit. Following this study of the Son in relation to his Father and the Spirit, we'll then consider four lines of application to our own lives, ministries, and relationships. May God grant eyes to see, ears to hear, minds to comprehend, hearts to embrace, and wills to live out what we see in Jesus.

THE SON IN RELATION TO THE FATHER

Two characteristics of the Son's relationship to the Father stand out in Scripture, and we will give attention to each, though greater focus will be given to the first. Without question, the whole framework of the earthly life, work, ministry, and mission of the Son was one in which the Son sought to do the will of the Father. Hence, the Son's submission to the leadership, authority, and headship of his Father must be given careful consideration if we are to understand how the Father and Son relate. Here, we'll focus on the headship of the Father over the Son in the Son's incarnate mission, and also in his relationship with the Father in eternity past and eternity future. We'll see, in short, that the Son in fact is the *eternal Son* of the *eternal Father,* and hence, the Son stands in a relationship of eternal submission under the authority of his Father. The second characteristic of this Father-Son relationship, one much more commonly seen and discussed, is the intimate and profound love each has for the other. The Father loves his Son dearly, and the Son loves his Father with equal fervor. We'll see and marvel at the fact that while the Father and Son are in a relationship marked by eternal authority and submission, yet they exhibit unqualified love for each other. To these two characteristics we now turn.

The Son Is Under the Headship or Authority of the Father

In 1 Corinthians 11:3 Paul writes, "But I want you to understand that the head of every man is Christ, the head of a wife is her husband, and *the head of Christ is God.*" Without question, the Son stands under the authority, or, if you will, the headship of the Father. In this chapter (1 Corinthians 11) where Paul is about to deal with the importance of women acknowledging the headship of men in the community of faith by wearing head coverings, he prefaces his remarks by describing authority and submission in human relations as a reflection of the authority and submission that exist in the eternal Godhead. God (the Father) is the head of Christ, says Paul.

A word often used by early church theologians for the evident authority structure of the Father-Son relationship in the Godhead is *taxis,* which means "ordering." There is an ordering in the Godhead, a "built-in" structure of authority and submission that marks a significant respect in which the Persons of the Godhead are distinguished from one another. Surely, they are not distinct in essence, for each shares fully the identically same divine nature. Their distinction, rather, is constituted, in part, by *taxis*—the ordering of Father, Son, and Holy Spirit within the Godhead. The order is not random or arbitrary; it is not Spirit first, Son second, and Father third, nor is it any way other than the one way that the early church, reflecting Scripture itself (Matt. 28:19), insisted on: Father, Son, and Holy Spirit. It seems that 1 Corinthians 11:3 suggests this and then applies this same *taxis* to God-designed human relationships. For all eternity, the order establishes that God is the head of Christ; within the created sphere, there is an ordering such that Christ is the head of man; and within human relationships, the order establishes that man is the head of woman. Intrinsic to God's own nature is a fundamental *taxis,* and he has so designed creation to reflect his own being, his own internal and eternal relationships, in part, through created and designed relationships of *taxis.*

The egalitarian movement in our evangelical circles, sadly, seeks to deny this very *taxis,* both in God's trinitarian structure of relations and in those elements of the created order that he made to reflect the same kind of *taxis.* Surely this must be grieving in God's sight. To insist on egalitarian relationships where God has designed structures of authority and submission is to indicate, even implicitly, that we just don't like the very authority-submission structures that characterize who God is, and that characterize his good and wise created design for us. But when we see that this structure of authority-submission pictures God himself—that the members of the Trinity exist eternally as equal in their essence but distinct in the *taxis* that marks their distinct roles—then we realize that what we have chafed at is, at heart, the very nature of God himself. Seeing God as he is, then, may provide for us a stronger basis to look afresh at human relationships of authority and submission, and to see in them the wisdom and goodness that God intended. We should therefore look more closely at just how the Son submits to his Father, and from this we may comprehend better how human relationships may best be understood and lived.[1]

1. *The Son's submission to the Father during his incarnation and earthly mission.* We begin this investigation of the Son's submission to the Father at a place where there is agreement among nearly all who consider this subject. Even if people question whether the Son submits eternally to the Father, the evidence is overwhelming and absolutely clear that in the incarnate life and ministry of Jesus, he lived in submission to the Father. That is, Jesus sought in all he planned, said, and did to obey his Father, in full submission to the Father's will. Consider just some of the evidence.

The Gospel of John, in particular, makes much of Jesus' constant desire to obey his Father. In a fascinating account, Jesus said to some religious leaders who were with him, "You are from below; I am from above. You are of this world; I am not of this world" (John 8:23). Here, Jesus established his preexistence, prior to the incarnation, and he implied by this not only that he came from above but that he was, in his very nature, uncreated and divine. Given this emphasis on his intrinsic deity (an emphasis he often makes, especially in John's Gospel), other statements by Jesus are quite astonishing. A few verses later, Jesus said, "When you have lifted up the Son of Man, then you will know that I am he, and that *I do nothing on my own authority,* but *speak just as the Father taught me.* And he who sent me is with me. He has not left me alone, for *I always do the things that are pleasing to him*" (John 8:28-29). And the amazement in this text only continues, as some come to believe in him, and he says to them, "If you abide in my word, you are truly my disciples, and you will know the truth, and the truth will set you free" (John 8:31-32).

What do we learn from this account? First, the very same Jesus who claims implicitly to be God (John 8:23) then proceeds to describe himself as doing nothing by his own authority, speaking only what the Father teaches him, and doing only and always what pleases the Father (vv. 28-29). How amazing this is. Jesus is God, but Jesus obeys God. Jesus is not of this world, but in this world Jesus refuses to speak or act on his own initiative, choosing rather to do only what pleases his Father. Clearly, the only way to make sense of this is to see that the eternal Son of the Father is both *"God the Son"* and *"God the Son."* That is, as eternally divine and not of this world, he is *God* the Son, but as under the authority of his Father, and as the eternal Son of the Father, he is God the *Son.* Both are true of Christ, and that both are true is a wonder indeed. One might think that if he is God, then he wouldn't be under anyone's authority, or if he is a Son, then he couldn't be fully divine. But divine he is, and a Son he is. As God the Son, he submits to God his Father.

Second, the level of Christ's submission to the Father is nearly unbelievable. Hear again his words: "I do *nothing* on my own authority . . . I *always* do the things that are pleasing to him" (John 8:28-29). And of course, we know that these claims must be exactly correct, because Jesus went to the cross absolutely sinless, having done nothing other than the will of his Father (cf. 2 Cor. 5:21; Heb. 4:15). The level of Jesus' submission to the Father is complete, comprehensive, all-inclusive, and absolute. There are no exceptions to his submission and obedience, for he never once sinned, throughout all of his life.

Third, directly following these statements of Jesus' absolute obedience to the Father, that he never spoke anything by his own initiative and always and only did what was pleasing to the Father, Jesus has the audacity (or so it would appear!) to instruct on the subject of freedom! Abide in his words, he told those who believed in him, and they would become disciples of his, and they would know the truth, and the truth would set them free. Live as Jesus has lived before the Father, abiding in his truth and speaking only what the Father has taught them, and they will be like Jesus, knowing the truth and entering into true freedom. It appears, then, that we need to learn something about the nature of true freedom.[2] Freedom is not what our culture tells us it is. Freedom is *not* my deciding, from the urges and longings of my sinful nature, to do *what* I want to do, *when* I want to do it, *how* I want to do it, *with whom* I want to do it. According to the Bible, that is bondage, not freedom. Rather, true freedom is living as Jesus lived, for he is the freest human being who ever lived. In fact, he is the only *fully free* human being who has ever lived, and one day we will be set free fully when we always and only do the will of God. So, what is freedom? Amazingly, Jesus' answer is this: Freedom is submitting—submitting fully to the will of God, to the words of God, and to the work that God calls us to do.

Another glimpse of the pervasive and passionate submission of Jesus to the Father is seen in John 4. Recall the episode where Jesus was speaking to the Samaritan woman. His disciples had gone away to get food and they came back and realized that Jesus had not eaten anything while they were away. They were sure he must be very hungry and asked him if he wanted something to eat. Jesus responded that he had food to eat that they did not know about, and they puzzled over this (John 4:32-33). Jesus then said to them, "My food is to do the will of him who sent me and to accomplish his work" (v. 34). That is, my "food," my sustenance, what nourishes me, what fuels me, what drives me, Jesus says, is doing the will of my Father.

This idea that Jesus' food was doing the will of his Father should bring to mind another episode from his life. In his temptation, when he had fasted from all foods for forty days, we read that the devil came to him and challenged him, saying, "If you are the Son of God, command these stones to become loaves of bread" (Matt. 4:3). In keeping with his entire life's pattern of thought, behavior, and conviction, Jesus answered Satan, "Man shall not live by bread alone, but by every word that comes from the mouth of God" (v. 4). In other words, more than anything else, Jesus cared about doing what the Father wanted him to do. Even after fasting forty days, he would not eat until his Father had indicated to him that the fast was over and that the time had come for him to eat. Jesus lived his life in abject submission to his Father, and in this he was both fully free and fully man. And in this he also was fully God.

2. *The Son's submission to the Father in eternity past.* What about Jesus' submission to the Father prior to the incarnation? Some acknowledge that Jesus submitted to the Father during the incarnation but reject the notion that he also submitted to the Father in eternity past. And some also resist the notion that his submission continues after the incarnation into eternity future. In other words, some see the Son's submission to the Father as true only for the purpose of the incarnational mission.[3] It is not difficult to see why some find the Son's eternal submission to the Father an objectionable concept. For if the Son eternally submits to the Father, this would indicate that authority and submission are eternal realities. And if so, would it not stand to reason that when God creates the world he

would fashion it in a way that reflects these eternal structures? And would it not make sense, then, that the authority-submission structures in marriage and in church leadership are meant to be reflections of the authority and submission in the relations of the Persons of the Godhead? But because some find the very notion of authority and submission objectionable—at least objectionable in these two spheres of human relationships—they clearly resist seeing this relational dynamic as true of the eternal relations within the Godhead.[4] But is this what Scripture indicates? Does the Bible give any indication whether the Son's submission to the Father took place in eternity past and eternity future as well as during his incarnational mission? And has the church understood their relationship in these terms? Let us consider some of the evidence for the Son's submission to the Father in eternity past.

First, consider some of the key biblical support for the Son's submission to the Father prior to and apart from the incarnation. I would argue that 1 Corinthians 11:3 offers a truth-claim about the relationship between the Father and Son that reflects an eternal verity. That God is the head of Christ is not presented here as an ad hoc relationship for Christ's mission during the incarnation. It is rather stated as an absolute fact regarding this relationship. God is the head of Christ. The Father has authority over the Son. There is a relationship of authority and submission in the very Godhead on which the other authority-submission relationships of Christ and man, and man and woman, depend. The *taxis* of God's headship over his Son accounts for the presence of *taxis* in man's relationship with Christ and the woman's relationship with man.

In addition, John's Gospel mentions more than thirty times the fact that Jesus was sent by the Father to accomplish his mission, and in some of these places it is very clear that the sending took place before the Son became incarnate. His very coming to earth was itself in obedience to the Father. Hear, for example, the familiar words of John 3:16 and 17: "For God so loved the world, that he gave his only

Son, that whoever believes in him should not perish but have eternal life. For God did not send his Son into the world to condemn the world, but in order that the world might be saved through him." The Father *sent* the Son into the world to be the very Lamb of God, sent for the forgiveness of sins. The Son obeyed the Father in eternity past, then, by saying, essentially, "Yes, Father, I will accept the mission you have designed for me, to take on human flesh and to bear the guilt and punishment of human sin." Or again Jesus said, "Do you say of him whom the Father consecrated and sent into the world, 'You are blaspheming,' because I said, 'I am the Son of God'?" (John 10:36). Clearly, the Father both consecrated the Son for the mission he planned for him, and then sent the Son into the world to fulfill what he had designed. For this to be meaningful and make sense, we must understand both the consecration and the sending of the Son as happening prior to the incarnation and therefore as being in the design of God in eternity past. Again, Jesus said, "For I have come down from heaven, not to do my own will but the will of him who sent me" (John 6:38). Again we see that Jesus' obedience to the Father occurred prior to his incarnation, and this prior obedience accounts for the very incarnation itself.

Another text, this one from 1 Peter, indicates that the Father planned and purposed to send his Son into the world even before creation itself. Peter writes, "Knowing that you were ransomed from the futile ways inherited from your forefathers, not with perishable things such as silver and gold, but with the precious blood of Christ, like that of a lamb without blemish or spot. He [Christ] was foreknown before the foundation of the world but was made manifest in the last times for your sake, who through him are believers in God, who raised him from the dead and gave him glory, so that your faith and hope are in God" (1 Pet. 1:18-21). The key phrase, of course, is Peter's reference to Christ having been foreknown by the Father before the foundation of the world. Foreknowledge here does not mean merely knowing ahead of time what is going to happen. Of course God has foreknowledge in that sense. But more than that, to foreknow is to choose one for some certain purpose,[5] to know in the sense of favoring this particular one upon whom you choose to bestow some privileged service or calling. Thus, God had established his Son as the one who would bring everything into subjection under his feet, as the one who would be raised above all of creation and given the name that is above every name. His Son would be given glory (v. 21) through his suffering, death, and subsequent resurrection and exaltation. But when did the Father make this prior decision to choose his Son for this most favored of all callings? "Before the foundation of the world" is the answer given by Peter. This requires, then, an authority-submission relationship in eternity past, one in which the Father chooses and sends, and the Son submits and comes.

Therefore, as we consider the incarnational mission of Christ, with the Son expressing his own submission to the Father with words such as, "I do nothing on my own authority, but speak just as the Father taught me" (John 8:28), we see that this same relationship of submission to the Father was true in eternity past, even before the creation of the world. The submission of the Son in the incarnation is but a reflection of the eternal relationship that has always been true with his Father. The Son always seeks to do the will of the Father, and this is true eternally.

Second, lest one think that this understanding of the Son's "prior" submission to the Father is a new idea in the history of the church, we should note that while the early church clearly embraced the full essential equality of the three trinitarian Persons (because each of the three divine Persons possesses fully and simultaneously the identically same eternal divine nature), nonetheless the church has always affirmed likewise the priority of the Father over the Son and Spirit. Since this priority cannot rightly be understood in terms of essence or nature (lest one fall into Arian subordinationism), it must be understood in terms of relationship.[6] As

Augustine affirmed, the distinction of Persons is constituted precisely by the differing relations among them, in part manifested by
the inherent authority of the Father and inherent submission of the
Son. This is seen most clearly in the eternal Father-Son relationship
in which the Father is eternally the *Father* of the Son, and the Son is
eternally the *Son* of the Father. Consider how Augustine discusses
both the essential equality of the Father and Son, and the mission
of the Son who was sent, in eternity past, to obey and carry out the
will of the Father:

> If however the reason why the Son is said to have been sent by
> the Father is simply that the one is the Father and the other the
> Son then there is nothing at all to stop us believing that the *Son*
> *is equal to the Father* and consubstantial and co-eternal, and yet that
> the Son is sent by the Father. *Not because one is greater and the other*
> *less, but because one is the Father and the other the Son;* one is the beget-
> ter, the other begotten; the first is the one from whom the sent
> one is; the other is the one who is from the sender. For the Son
> is from the Father, not the Father from the Son. In the light of
> this we can now perceive that *the Son is not just said to have been sent*
> *because the Word became flesh, but that he was sent in order for the Word*
> *to become flesh,* and by his bodily presence to do all that was writ-
> ten. That is, we should understand that *it was not just the man who*
> *the Word became that was sent, but that the Word was sent to become man.*
> For he was *not sent in virtue of some disparity of power or substance or*
> *anything in him that was not equal to the Father,* but in virtue of the
> Son being from the Father, not the Father being from the Son.[7]

Notice two observations from Augustine's statement. First,
Augustine sees no disparity between affirming, on the one hand, the
full *equality* of the Son to the Father, and on the other hand, the Son's
eternal position as *from* the Father, with the responsibility of carrying out the will of the Father. The claim of some egalitarians[8] that
the functional subordination of the Son would entail his essential
inferiority to the Father is here denied by Augustine. Second, notice

that Augustine denies the egalitarian claim that all subordination of the Son to the Father rests fully in the Son's incarnate state. To the contrary, Augustine affirms that "the Son is not just said to have been sent because the Word became flesh, but that *he was sent in order for the Word to become flesh."* In other words, the sending of the Son occurred in eternity past in order that the eternal Word, sent from on high from the Father, might take on human flesh and then continue his role of carrying out the will of his Father.

As P. T. Forsyth writes, the beauty of the Son's simultaneous equality with and obedience to the Father expresses the willing service God intends his people to render. Forsyth asserts that "subordination is *not* inferiority, and it *is* Godlike. The principle is imbedded in the very cohesion of the eternal Trinity and it is inseparable from the unity, fraternity and true equality of men. It is not a mark of inferiority to be subordinate, to have an authority, to obey. It is divine."[9] And in another place, Forsyth makes clear that the Son's obedience to the Father was indeed an eternal obedience, rendered by an eternal equal, constituting an eternal subordination of the Son to do the will of the Father. He writes:

> Father and Son co-exist, co-equal in the Spirit of holiness, i.e., of perfection. But Father and Son is a relation inconceivable except the Son be obedient to the Father. The perfection of the Son and the perfecting of his holy work lay, not in his suffering but in his obedience. And, as he was eternal Son, it meant an eternal obedience. . . . But obedience is not conceivable without some form of subordination. Yet in his very obedience the Son was co-equal with the Father; the Son's yielding will was no less divine than the Father's exigent will. Therefore, in the very nature of God, subordination implies no inferiority.[10]

Third, the egalitarian denial of any eternal submission of the Son to the Father makes it impossible to answer the question why it was the "Son" and not the "Father" or "Spirit" who was sent to become incarnate. John Thompson has indicated a trend in much modern trinitarian discussion to separate Christology from trinitarian formulations. He writes that "Christology and the Trinity were virtually divorced. It was both stated and assumed that any one of the three persons could become incarnate. . . . There was thus only an accidental relation between the economy of revelation and redemption and the eternal triune being of God."[11] It appears that contemporary egalitarianism is vulnerable also to this criticism. Since, in their understanding, nothing *in God* grounds the Son being the Son of the Father, and since every aspect of the Son's earthly submission to the Father is divorced altogether from any *eternal relation* that exists between the Father and Son, there simply is no reason why the *Father* should send the *Son*. In Thompson's words, it appears that the egalitarian view would permit "any one of the three persons" to become incarnate. And yet we have clear and abundant scriptural revelation that the Son came down out of heaven to do the will of his Father. This sending is not *ad hoc*. In eternity, the Father commissioned the Son who then willingly laid aside the glory he had with the Father to come and purchase our pardon and renewal. Such glory is diminished if there is no eternal Father-Son relation on the basis of which the Father sends, the Son willingly comes, and the Spirit willingly empowers.

Fourth and last, even more basic is the question why the eternal names for "Father" and "Son" would be exactly *these* names. One must come to terms with the fact that God specifically revealed himself to us with the names "Father" and "Son" for the first and second Persons of the Trinity. Certainly these names carry connotations of authority and submission, as is confirmed by the Son's uniform declaration that he, the Son, sought only to do the will of his Father. Unless one is prepared to say that these names apply only to the incarnational relationship of the first and second Persons of the Trinity, in which case we simply don't know who these first and second Persons are eternally, we must admit that

God's self-revelation would indicate an identity of the Persons of Father and Son which also marks their respective roles. Authority and submission, then, seem clearly to be built into the eternal relationship of the Father and Son, by virtue of their being who they eternally are: God the Father, and God the Son.

3. *The Son's submission to the Father in eternity future.* What about eternity future? Do we have reason to think that the Son, having accomplished the mission that the Father sent him to do, will still be in submission to his Father in the ages to come? Consider first Paul's teaching of Christ's future reign over all things, when everything in heaven and earth is put in subjection under his feet:

> Then comes the end, when he [Christ] delivers the kingdom to God the Father after destroying every rule and every authority and power. For he [Christ] must reign until he has put all his enemies under his feet. The last enemy to be destroyed is death. For "God has put all things in subjection under his feet." But when it says, "all things are put in subjection," it is plain that he is excepted who put all things in subjection under him. When all things are subjected to him, then the Son himself will also be subjected to him who put all things in subjection under him, that God may be all in all (1 Cor. 15:24-28).

As we observed in the previous chapter, this passage indicates the preeminence of the Father even over the Son. The Son has his position over all of creation, bringing everything into subjection under his own feet, only because the Father has given all things to the Son. The Son, then, shows himself as the supreme victor and conqueror of all, including the conqueror of death itself, only because the Father has given him this highest of all callings and roles. In full acknowledgment of the Father's supremacy, the Son displays his submission to the Father by delivering up the kingdom that he gains to the Father, and then, remarkably, by subjecting himself also to his Father. Though all of creation is subject to him, he himself is subject to his Father. There is no question that this passage indicates the eternal future submission of the Son to the Father, in keeping with his submission to the Father both in the incarnation and in eternity past.

Surely this is confirmed by other indications from Scripture. For example, in Philippians 2, after Christ is presented as exalted above all, every knee will bow and every tongue will confess that Jesus Christ is Lord, "to the glory of God the Father" (Phil. 2:11). This parallels exactly what we have seen in 1 Corinthians 15. While the Son is exalted over all of creation, the Father himself is seen as preeminent over the Son. Similarly, in the grand heavenly scene portrayed by John in the Revelation, notice that after the Lamb who had been slain went up to him who sat on the throne and took the scroll to open its seals, we read, "And I heard every creature in heaven and on earth and under the earth and in the sea, and all that is in them, saying, 'To him who sits on the throne and to the Lamb be blessing and honor and glory and might forever and ever!'" (Rev. 5:13). Once again, while the Lamb is worshiped with him who is on the throne, so that the Father and the Son are seen equally and fully as God, yet the Son (i.e., the Lamb) approaches the throne at the right hand of him who sits on it, and the Son is distinguished from the one on the throne itself. In this scene picturing future worship in the ages to come, the Son is shown to be under the authority of the Father (for the Father gives him the scroll to open), while he is equal with the Father (for he is worshiped with the Father).

Clearly, then, Scripture teaches that Jesus' submission to the Father extends from eternity past to eternity future, and what we see in the incarnational mission of Christ over and over again is simply the manifestation, here and now, of what is eternally true in the relationship between the Father and the Son. While the Son eternally is *God* the Son, he always has been, was during the incarnation, and always will be, God the *Son* of God the *Father*. Authority and submission reside eternally in this Father-Son relationship, as taught clearly in Scripture and affirmed by the fathers of the church. As Colin Gunton has commented, reflecting on the portrayal of the future subjection of the Son to the Father in 1 Corinthians 15:28, this description has "implications for what we may say about the being of God eternally, and would seem to suggest a subordination of *taxis*—of ordering within the divine life— but not one of deity or regard. It is as truly divine to be the obedient self-giving Son as it is to be the Father who sends and the Spirit who renews and perfects."[12] We are enabled to see here something of what constitutes the beauty, the wisdom, and the goodness of the relations among the trinitarian Persons when we see the Son at work accomplishing the will of the Father. It is the nature of God both to exert authority and to obey in submission. And since this is the eternal nature of God, we may know that it is beautiful and it is good, and because of this, we are prompted to marvel a bit more at the glory that is our Triune God.

The Son in Loving Relationship with the Father

Is there a connection between the first and second of the two themes we are discussing here, the themes of the Son's eternal submission to the Father, and now, the love relationship between the Son and the Father? Some might say that if the first theme is true, the second simply cannot follow. That is, if the relationship between the Father and Son is marked by eternal authority and submission, then this precludes any real and genuine love between the two of them. How could it be, some would reason, that one who is eternally under the authority of Another could genuinely love the one over him? And how could genuine love be given by one in authority to the one in a subordinate position under him?

If our intuitions would lead us to think along these lines, we will soon learn from Scripture that our intuitions have failed us yet again. In fact, not only does the Son express his absolute and unqualified allegiance to the Father in strict obedience to his every word and command, the Son does so out of a deep and abiding love for his Father. In short, the Son's *submission to the Father,* and his *love for the Father,* are inseparable.

Consider these words from Jesus regarding his love for his Father: *"I do as the Father has commanded me,* so that the world may know that *I love the Father"* (John 14:31). Far from begrudging the obedience that the Father required of him, Jesus accepted it gladly. Recall John 4:34 where Jesus said, "My food is to do the will of him who sent me and to accomplish his work." And now in John 14:31, Jesus makes clear that his obedience is not only rendered gladly and with earnest delight, in fact his obedience is rendered out of a deep and abiding love for his Father. He wants others to know of his love for the Father through the very obedience and allegiance that he so gladly and uncompromisingly performs.

And of course, the love relationship flows in the other direction as well, from Father to Son. And in this other direction, the obedience of the Son is still very much in the center of the love that is manifested. Consider John 15:9-10: *"As the Father has loved me,* so have I loved you. Abide in my love. If you keep my commandments, you will abide in my love, just as *I have kept my Father's commandments and abide in his love."* Of course, the appeal Jesus is making here is primarily for the disciples to abide in his (the Son's) love through keeping the commandments of the Son. But, in order for them to know that the connection between obedience and abiding in the love of the one whom they are to obey is not new, or strange, or particular only to them, he makes clear that this is exactly how things have worked between himself (the Son) and his Father. "I have kept my Father's commandments," says Jesus, and precisely *because* of this I "abide in his love." At the heart of the love relationship between the Son and the Father, with love shown from each to the other, are the obedience of the Son to the Father and the authority of the Father over the Son. This obedience of the Son at one and

the same time expresses the Son's love for the Father and is the basis
by which the Son abides in the Father's love for him. So, yes, the
Son loves the Father, but this love is shown as the Son obeys the
Father, and in no way contrary to this. And, yes, the Father loves the
Son, but the Son abides in this fatherly love only as he obeys every
command and word given him from the Father. Love and obedience, then, run together in an inseparable union in this relationship
between God the Father and God the Son.

Any notion that true love between the Father and Son could be
carried out only by "functional equals" is shown to be fully misguided by the testimony of Jesus himself. In fact, just the opposite
is the case. The love relationship between the Father and Son is carried out within the structure of authority and submission, of command and obedience. Jesus often tells of his love for the Father and
his Father's love for him. But all such discussions clearly and constantly highlight the authority of the Father and the obedience of the
Son. Yes, the Son loves his Father, and the Father loves his Son. But
this love relationship is empty, according to Jesus, apart from the
framework of the Father's authority and the Son's submission.
When seen correctly, then, these two themes of Jesus' relationship
with the Father—the authority of the Father and the obedience of
the Son; and the love relationship between the Father and the
Son—unite as one.

THE SON IN RELATION TO THE SPIRIT

We must now consider the Son's relationship to the Spirit. And on
this subject, we have a very interesting set of New Testament data
to examine. What we find are two themes that appear, at first glance,
to be in conflict, two themes that simply do not easily join together.
On the one hand, Jesus follows the lead of the Spirit and relies on
the Spirit, and so is shown to *submit to the Spirit* in order to accomplish his mission. But on the other hand, Jesus has *authority over the
Spirit,* so that as Jesus gives the Spirit to those who believe on him,

the Spirit comes to "glorify me," says Jesus (John 16:14). This raises the question, then, of who has authority over whom? Is this a reciprocal relationship of authority and submission? Does this illustrate the kind of "mutual submission" that many in the egalitarian movement urge us to adopt? Just how should we understand and evaluate these two sets of New Testament teachings about the relationship between Jesus and the Spirit?

Jesus' Submission to the Spirit—to Fulfill His Role as the Spirit-anointed Messiah

Jesus lived his life as a fully human man in submission to the Spirit. This is a theme that both is anticipated in Old Testament prophecies and is shown to be true in the Gospel accounts of Jesus' life and ministry; but it is a theme far too little appreciated by many evangelicals. If asked, "How did Jesus live in full obedience to the Father?" many evangelicals would reply, "Jesus lived his life of sinless obedience out of the power of his divine nature." While it is absolutely true that Jesus was both fully God and fully man, the proposed answer does not reflect what the Scriptures teach.

Consider, for example, Isaiah 11:1-2:

> There shall come forth a shoot from the stump of Jesse,
>   and a branch from his roots shall bear fruit.
> And the Spirit of the LORD shall rest upon him,
>   the Spirit of wisdom and understanding,
>   the Spirit of counsel and might,
>   the Spirit of knowledge and the fear of the LORD.

Does it not seem odd that if Jesus (the coming "shoot from the stump of Jesse") lived his life of obedience by the power of his divine nature, we would read that when he comes, "the Spirit of the LORD shall rest upon him"? After all, what can the Spirit of God add to the divine nature of Jesus? The answer, of course, is "nothing." Jesus' divine nature is omnipotent, omniscient, and in every way infinite and eternal in the fullness of perfection. Furthermore, Jesus' divine nature is the identically same divine nature as the divine nature of the Spirit and of the Father. So, why should Jesus be given the Spirit?

But this is not the only question that Isaiah 11:1-2 raises. Think particularly about what is said in verse 2. Here we read that the Spirit who will rest on Jesus will be the Spirit of wisdom, understanding, counsel, might, knowledge, and the fear of the LORD. Does this not indicate that the wisdom that Jesus will exhibit in his earthly ministry as the Son of David, from the stump of Jesse, will be wisdom wrought in him *by the Spirit?* Are not the understanding, the counsel, the might, the knowledge, and the fear of the LORD, that Jesus manifests in his life and teaching, the qualities elicited through him *by the Spirit?* In fact, Isaiah 11:2 is strikingly similar to Galatians 5:22-23, where the "fruit of the Spirit" (love, joy, peace, patience, kindness, goodness, faithfulness, gentleness, self-control) are the qualities of the Spirit himself worked out in and through our very characters and actions. So too with Jesus, the Spirit of the Lord will work in and through him to produce the very character qualities and capacities that Isaiah 11:2 highlights.

One of the first things we read about Jesus in his public ministry has to do with his following the lead of the Spirit and living his life in the power of the Spirit. Luke tells us that after his baptism, "Jesus, *full of the Holy Spirit,* returned from the Jordan and was *led by the Spirit* in the wilderness for forty days, being tempted by the devil" (Luke 4:1-2a). Why mention the Spirit in such ways unless the very places that Jesus would go and his very empowerment for obedience were linked to the Spirit being in him and working through him? Jesus prevailed over the deceitful temptations of the devil, and we read further, "Jesus returned in the power of the Spirit to Galilee" (Luke 4:14). Luke wants us to know that Jesus is living his life by the power of the Spirit, obeying the Father and resisting temptation as the Spirit works in him.

Among the first places Jesus went in Galilee was to his home town, Nazareth, where he entered the synagogue on the Sabbath and read Scripture for them. When handed the book of Isaiah, he "found the place where it was written,

> "'The Spirit of the Lord is upon me,
>   because he has anointed me
>   to proclaim good news to the poor.
> He has sent me to proclaim liberty to the captives
>   and recovering of sight to the blind,
>   to set at liberty those who are oppressed,
> to proclaim the year of the Lord's favor'" (Luke 4:18-19, quoting from Isa. 61:1-2).

When Jesus had finished reading, he handed the book back to the attendant, sat down, and said, "Today this Scripture has been fulfilled in your hearing" (Luke 4:21). It is astonishing that Jesus not only knew that he was the Spirit-anointed Messiah, but he knew that the fact of his being Spirit-anointed was so crucial that he selected this text to read—and announced its fulfillment.

Many more Scriptures show how Jesus lived his life, carried out his mission, performed his miracles, and in every way obeyed the Father—all by the power of the Spirit. Perhaps just one further text will be especially helpful. When Peter preached the gospel to Cornelius in Acts 10, he started with a brief summary of Jesus' life and ministry. In light of our present discussion, look carefully at just how Peter chose to summarize the way in which Jesus lived his life. Speaking of Jesus' ministry, beginning from Galilee after his baptism, Peter spoke about "how God *anointed Jesus* of Nazareth with the *Holy Spirit and with power.* He went about doing good and healing all who were oppressed by the devil, for God was *with* him" (Acts 10:38). Rather than saying that Jesus went about doing good and healing by the power of his own divine nature (which, of course, Jesus had!) all who were oppressed, Peter instead appeals to Jesus' Spirit-anointing as the basis by which Jesus lived his life, performed his miracles, and completed the mission given him by the Father. And Peter's reference to Jesus being anointed "with the Holy Spirit and with power" is an unmistakable parallel to what Jesus had said to Peter (and the other disciples) in Acts 1:8: "you will receive power when the Holy Spirit has come upon you." As Jesus lived his (fully human) life in the power of the Holy Spirit, so at Pentecost, the disciples of Jesus would likewise receive the Holy Spirit and his power, by which they would live their lives and carry out the calling given them. Although Jesus was fully God, as a man he chose to rely not on his own divine nature but on the power of the Spirit. In this way, he lived his life as an example for us (1 Pet. 2:21-22), and fulfilled the perfect obedience that Adam had failed to accomplish.

Yes, Jesus lived his life in the power of the Spirit, for Jesus came as the second Adam, the seed of Abraham, the son of David, that is, a human being who needed supernatural enablement to live the human life of obedience and sacrifice that the Father had ordained for him to carry out. In short, the "human Jesus" needed the Spirit in ways that the "divine Jesus" simply did not and could not need him. But since Jesus came as "one of us," as it were, as a full human being who lived our life and died in our place, he came in need of the Spirit of God to empower his life, ministry, obedience, miracles, and all that he did in obedience to the Father.

Understanding that Jesus lived his life as a human being, in reliance on the Holy Spirit, is important in making sense of how Jesus, the second Person of the Trinity, could submit himself fully to the Spirit—the Spirit whom he later would say would "glorify me" (John 16:14). As a man, Jesus *submitted fully to the Spirit*, even though in terms of rank, within the Trinity, Jesus has *authority over the Spirit*. For the sake of his mission, he humbled himself. In taking on our human nature, he submitted to the very one over whom he has rightful authority.

This explains some aspects of Jesus' life that otherwise are inexplicable. It explains, for example, how it is, as we read in Luke 2:40, 52, that Jesus "grew" in wisdom. How can this be? He certainly cannot grow in wisdom in his divine nature, so what must this mean? Perhaps we can think of it this way: in the consciousness of the God-man, the person Jesus Christ of Nazareth, he accepted the limitations of what it is to be a human, in order to grow in understanding, to grow in wisdom, as the Spirit in him would help him see things more clearly and understand God's Word with greater clarity and greater forcefulness as he grew older. In this sense, then, he was like any child born; like other babies he did not know everything at birth but had to grow in his understanding and in wisdom as he aged and matured. We should not think of Jesus lying in the manger in Bethlehem, looking up at the stars of the heavens and contemplating the physics of the universe he created! Rather, that baby in the manger, though uniquely the God-man, had accepted the confines of human limitations in order to live life as one of us.

In accepting these human limitations, however, Jesus did not discard or give up any attributes of deity. To think so is to deny the full deity of Christ and to entertain a view judged by the church as a heresy. Rather, while Jesus was fully God, and as such retained all the infinite and eternal attributes possessed by his divine nature, he accepted the limitation or restriction of the use (or expression, or manifestation) of certain of his divine attributes in order to live life fully as a man. After all, Jesus could not really have experienced life as we know it, or lived life as authentically human, if, for example, he was omniscient in his own consciousness as the person, Jesus Christ of Nazareth. While his divine nature continued to possess the attribute of omniscience, Jesus accepted the limitation of not having access to this infinite knowledge so that he could live as we live, and grow in wisdom and understanding, through the hard work of learning, by the power of the Spirit. This explains, then, what Jesus says concerning the hour of the second coming, which "no one knows, not even the angels in heaven, *nor the Son,* but only the Father" (Mark 13:32). Arius, of course, thought that this text supported his contention, against Athanasius, that Jesus was not God. The problem with Arius's view, simply put, is that so much evidence stands against him on this issue. Scripture is replete with teaching supporting the full deity of the Son, and thankfully Athanasius was persuasive when this issue was debated and decided at the Council of Nicea. Yet this text does say that the Son does not know something that the Father knows. How are we to understand this statement by Christ, since we accept that he was in nature fully God?

It seems that the answer must be that Jesus Christ, as a man, accepted the limitations of his human existence, including the limited knowledge that goes with living life as a finite human being. In his divine nature, he retained omniscience, but in the consciousness of Jesus, the God-man, he accepted a restricted knowledge so that he would have to trust his heavenly Father. He had to live by faith. He had to grow. He had to study. He had to, as Hebrews puts it, be "made perfect [i.e., mature]" (Heb. 5:9). He grew in these ways through the things he suffered and through the things that he learned. "He learned obedience through what he suffered" (v. 8). That is, Jesus learned little by little through life to obey increasingly difficult demands of his Father until he would become ready for the ultimate demand of going to the cross—which, even at that point, was excruciatingly difficult. How else do we explain Jesus in the garden sweating, as it were, drops of blood, three times crying out to the Father, "My Father, if it be possible, let this cup pass from me" (Matt. 26:39). To fail to see how enormously difficult this act of obedience was for Jesus is to miss the obvious. How incredibly, excruciatingly painful was this obedience. How did he arrive at the place where now, at this time, he was able to obey, even though his obedience was so very hard? He was prepared to accept this, the biggest of all challenges, because of tests of faith along the way. He "learned obedience" not by being disobedient and moving from disobedi-

ence to obedience (recall Heb. 4:15), but rather by being obedient
in ever more difficult tasks, demands, and challenges until the ultimate test had come. As a man, Jesus submitted to the Spirit, grew
in wisdom, learned to obey the Father in increasingly difficult ways,
and in all he did and said, he lived his life in the power of the Spirit.

*Jesus' Authority over the Spirit—in His Role as the
Son of the Father*

This same Jesus who submitted to the Spirit, who lived his life in
the power of the Spirit, also gave clear expression to his authority
over the Spirit. Scripture's teaching here is instructive in two important respects. First, Jesus made clear that although he had submitted to the Spirit in his life as the incarnate Son of the Father, the
order of relationship between himself and the Spirit, nevertheless,
was fundamentally the reverse. In John 16, Jesus spoke to his disciples about the coming Holy Spirit, and said, "I still have many things
to say to you, but you cannot bear them now. When the Spirit of
truth comes, he will guide you into all the truth, for he will not
speak on his own authority, but whatever he hears he will speak, and
he will declare to you the things that are to come. He will glorify
me, for he will take what is mine and declare it to you" (John 16:12-
14). In language strikingly similar to what Jesus had regularly said
about himself and the Father, he now speaks of the Spirit in relation
to him. Regarding his relation to the Father, you'll recall that Jesus
had said things such as, "I have come down from heaven, not to do
my own will but the will of him [the Father] who sent me" (John
6:38); "I do nothing on my own authority, but speak just as the
Father taught me" (John 8:28); and "I glorified you [the Father] on
earth, having accomplished the work that you gave me to do" (John
17:4). Now, in parallel fashion, Jesus says that the Spirit who is coming will not speak on his own authority but will speak what *Jesus* tells
him to speak. Just as Jesus glorified the Father in all he did, the Spirit
who comes will glorify *Jesus*. Interestingly, Jesus does *not* say, "Just

as I spoke only what the Father taught me, and just as I glorified the Father, so the Spirit, when he comes, likewise will only speak what the Father teaches him, for he will glorify the Father." No, the direct lines of authority and submission here run between the Spirit and the Son, not the Spirit and the Father. Although Jesus submitted fully to the Spirit in his incarnate life, still, the Spirit's eternal role is to uphold the will and the word of the Son; in his coming, the Spirit seeks in all he does to glorify Jesus.

Second, however, the relationship of authority and submission between the Son and the Spirit is set in a broader trinitarian context in several biblical passages. Consider, for example, another of Jesus' statements about the future coming of the Holy Spirit: "These things I have spoken to you while I am still with you. But the Helper, the Holy Spirit, *whom the Father will send in my name,* he will teach you all things and bring to your remembrance all that I have said to you" (John 14:25-26). So the Spirit, in his coming, will come *in the name of Jesus,* but he will be *sent from the Father* in order to bring to the disciples' remembrance what *Jesus has taught them.* Clearly, then, the Father has primacy in what is pictured here, for the Spirit is sent from the Father. But even though the Father sends the Spirit, the Spirit is sent not to teach or remind concerning the words of the Father, per se. Rather, the Father sends the Spirit in order for the Spirit to uphold the teaching of the Son.

This is made even clearer a few moments later when Jesus says, "But when the Helper comes, whom *I will send* to you *from the Father,* the Spirit of truth, who *proceeds from the Father,* he will bear witness *about me*" (John 15:26). How fascinating! And how instructive. With greater nuance here, Jesus explains that the Spirit comes as he (Jesus) sends him, yet Jesus sends the Spirit "from the Father." So, it must be the case that the ultimate Sender of the Spirit is the Father, and the subordinate Sender is the Son. Both the Father and the Son send the Spirit (recall "I will send," indicating that Jesus is the sender; and "who proceeds from the Father," indicating that the

Father is the sender, confirming what Jesus had said in John 14:26),
but the priority goes to the Father. Yet, while the Father is the primary Sender, the primary reason for the Spirit being sent is not to
bear witness of the Father, but to bear witness of the Son. Lines of
authority, of *taxis* within the Trinity, are being honored here in the
very precise language Jesus uses to explain the manner in which the
Holy Spirit will come. Jesus speaks as he does in order to guard the
primary place of the Father in devising and carrying out the entire
plan of salvation, which includes his sending the Son into the world
(John 6:38) and his sending the Spirit into the world (John 14:26).
Yet, in sending the Spirit, there seems clearly to be a two-fold sending. So, Jesus speaks of the Spirit "whom *I will send* to you *from the
Father.*" And the Spirit who comes *"proceeds from the Father."* The primary sending agent, then, is the Father, and the Father enjoins the
Son's participation in sending the Spirit, since the Spirit comes to
"bear witness *about me,"* as Jesus puts it.

One other text helps clarify this relationship of the Father and
Son with the Spirit. In Peter's sermon on the day of Pentecost,
explaining how the gathered believers had received the Holy Spirit
and had demonstrated such supernatural enablement, Peter speaks
about the death and resurrection of Christ, and then comments
regarding this risen Christ, "Being therefore exalted at the right
hand of God, and having *received from the Father* the promise of the
Holy Spirit, *he has poured out this* that you yourselves are seeing and
hearing" (Acts 2:33). The reader of the book of Acts will recall that
in the first chapter, Jesus had instructed his disciples to stay in
Jerusalem and to "wait for the promise of the Father" (Acts 1:4),
which was none other than that they would be "baptized with the
Holy Spirit not many days from now" (Acts 1:5). And now Peter,
in his sermon in Acts 2, recalls this "promise of the Father" that the
Father would give them the Holy Spirit, and so he says that they
have "received from the Father the promise of the Holy Spirit."
And of course, this connects fully with Peter's quoting of Joel

2:28ff., where God had promised (as he had in many other Old Testament texts) that one day he would send his Spirit on all the people of God (see Acts 2:16-21). But the precise way in which Peter states the fulfillment of this "promise of the Father" is as remarkable as it is instructive. Peter could simply have said that the Father poured forth the Spirit as he had long ago promised, and this would have been accurate. But he states with greater precision and nuance just how Jesus also figures into the sending of the Spirit. The Spirit comes as the Father sends him, to be sure. But the Spirit comes as the Father *first* gives the Spirit to the Son, and *then* as the Son "has poured out this [i.e., the Spirit] that you yourselves are seeing and hearing."

The Father and Son are two-fold Senders of the Spirit. The Father is primary and ultimate in this sending, yet the Son is the immediate and proximate Sender of the Spirit. The Father is seen, then, as supreme in authority in sending the Spirit, yet the Son, while under the authority of his Father, is in a position of authority over the Spirit. We have here, in this one historical incident, a beautiful picture of the eternal ordering within the very triune nature of God. The Father, as ultimate in authority over the Son and the Spirit, calls the Son forth from the grave and sets him at his own right hand. Then the Father, rather than giving the Spirit directly to the church, instead gives the gift of the Spirit to his Son so that the Son might have the honor and privilege to give the Spirit, from the Father, to those redeemed and called to new life through his work on their behalf. So the Son, having received this gift of the Spirit from the Father, then passes on this gift to the believers on the day of Pentecost.

By this, the Son is shown to be under the Father but over the Spirit. Although the Son is in submission to the Spirit in the incarnation, in his exaltation the Son "returns" to his place under the Father yet over the Spirit. So, the Spirit is the "Spirit of Jesus" (Acts 16:7), and the Spirit comes to "glorify" Jesus (John 16:14). As Paul expresses this principle, "no one speaking in the Spirit of God ever says 'Jesus is accursed!' and no one can say 'Jesus is Lord' except in the Holy Spirit" (1 Cor. 12:3). So here we have it: the Spirit is sent by the Son, as from the Father, that the Spirit might honor the Son, to the glory of the Father. Here we have a glorious mystery, rich with bases for worship, awe, and wonder. But these truths also call for thoughtful application, as we consider how the relationship of the Son to the Father and Spirit, respectively, should affect the way we live our lives and conduct our ministries.

APPLICATION FROM THE ROLE OF THE SON IN RELATION TO HIS FATHER AND THE SPIRIT

Although we will devote all of chapter six to how these truths should affect our own lives, consider with me briefly four lines of application that relate specifically to the Son's relationship with the Father and the Spirit, respectively.

1.   Marvel, as we have seen already and now see again, at the submission of the Son to the Father.

How remarkable that within the Godhead, not only is authority eternally exercised, but submission marks the relationship of the Son to the Father from eternity past to eternity future. How astonishing to realize that it is just as Godlike to submit gladly and joyfully to rightful authority as it is Godlike to exercise legitimate, rightful authority. Our tendency is to think of God as the one who has absolute authority, and of course this is true. But less known and little understood is the alternate truth that in God eternal submission to authority is also exercised. All of us, in one way or another, are in positions of submission. Certainly, wives to their husbands, children to their parents, congregations to their elders, employees to their employers, and citizens to their governments—all of us live in submission to one or more authority. Can we learn from Jesus what it means to be "Godlike" in submitting? Rather than despising authority, or even rather than yielding to authority with a grumbling and begrudging spirit, we learn from Jesus just what true submission looks like. May God grant us eyes to see the beauty of rightful authority and rightful submission, and may we seek to model our lives, by God's grace, more after the way Jesus lived always and only to please the Father.

2. Marvel at the submission of the incarnate Son to the Spirit over whom he, in his eternal existence as God, had rights of authority.

Marvel at the willingness, the humility, the condescension of the Son to submit to the leadership, the directives, the enablement of the Spirit. In particular, take to heart the level of the Son's submission to the Spirit when the Spirit led Jesus into the wilderness for forty days to be "tempted by the devil" (Luke 4:1-2). Stand amazed that the eternal Son of the Father, now incarnate as Jesus Christ of Nazareth, would obey and follow the Spirit's leading to face such a horrendous and difficult experience. That he did so faithfully and obediently is simply remarkable. And be amazed even more at the fact that Jesus went to the cross as "the eternal Spirit" led and empowered him to accomplish this greatest and most difficult of all callings (Heb. 9:14). The submission of the Son to the Spirit, the one over whom in his eternal existence as the Son of the Father he had rightful authority, is highly instructive and deeply humbling. What amazing humility, astonishing condescension, the Son has shown, and what a model he is for all who follow in his name.

3. Marvel at the unity and harmony within the triune relationships worked out in an authority-submission structure of relationship.

Imagine afresh a relationship in which those in authority and those in submission are on the same page, making their moves by the same playbook, fulfilling the same goal, supporting one another in the common mission, but all the while acknowledging who the Father, Son, and Spirit each is in this mutual work. Marvel at an authority-submission relationship worked out in unity and harmony, and then imagine what that would look like in our relationships with one another. Marvel at Jesus, the eternal Son of the eternal Father, accepting the Father's commandment that he come into this world to take on human flesh, live a perfect life in the power of the Spirit, and give his life a ransom for sinners. And honor this same Jesus, who having accomplished this work was exalted to the right hand of the Father and from there sent the Spirit, from the Father, that we might know the joy and freedom that his work for us on the cross has accomplished. Worship this Jesus who in the end will be honored as every knee bows and every tongue confesses that he is Lord, to the glory of God his Father (Phil. 2:9-11). And recall that this Jesus has understood and embraced from eternity past what he will live out into eternity future, that in all he does he seeks to bring honor to the Father. The unity and harmony, joined here with clear lines of authority and submission, defy the instincts of contemporary culture. Yet Jesus' life before his Father, in the power of the Spirit, calls us to a kind of life lived together of such greater joy and pleasure, as we seek to live, by God's grace, more like Jesus. Relations of authority and submission, lived out in unity and harmony—this is the model set for us by the Trinity, as expressed so beautifully in the life and ministry of Jesus.

4. Revel afresh at the extraordinary love of the Son for his Father and the Father for his Son, and consider from this Father-Son relationship the nature of true and perfect love.

Reflect again on these remarkable words from Jesus: "I do as the

Father has commanded me, so that the world may know that I love the Father" (John 14:31). And recall the extent of Jesus' obedience, as expressed by Paul in Philippians chapter 2: "he [Christ] humbled himself by becoming obedient to the point of death, even death on a cross" (Phil. 2:8). If Christ's obedience to the Father was the truest and necessary expression of the reality of his love for the Father, then the severity of what was asked of him and his willingness to obey at a cost beyond human comprehension indicate a love that is so great, so pure, so deep, and so passionate, that we can only grasp in miniscule part what this truest of all loves really is. But this much we can know: such love would never, could never, be love were it not for costly obedience. This is the hallmark of Jesus' love for the Father.

And what of the Father's love for his Son? As we have seen throughout this chapter and will have occasion to notice yet again, the Father takes such great joy and delight in "showing off" his Son. Jesus is, after all, his "beloved Son," and so we are to listen to and follow him. He favors his Son above all, and he grants his Son honor that is manifest over all. But is it love to command his Son to come and die? Is it love to require his Son to bear our sin and the Father's own wrath through the pain and agony of the cross? Of course, we know that "God so loved the world" when he sent his Son to die on our behalf (John 3:16). But did the Father love the Son in this action and in this sending? And the answer, amazingly, is yes, indeed. The Father showed his Son the highest honor by giving him the mission by which he would win the right to rule as King of kings and Lord of lords. The Father's very love for the Son led him to favor his Son (1 Pet. 1:20) for this highest of all privileges. Recall the logic of Paul's description of the obedience of Christ in Philippians 2. Yes, Christ humbled himself to the point of death, even death on a cross. But then Paul says, *"Therefore* God has highly exalted him and bestowed on him the name that is above every name" (Phil. 2:9). The Father's love for the Son led him to give to his Son, and to none other, the greatest of all tasks, that he might then grant him the highest of all names. The love of the Father for his Son is shown in the wisdom of his command and its blessing, ultimately, on the Son who would perfectly obey and then be honored. While this also is beyond our full comprehension, this much we can know—such love of the Father for the Son would never, could never, be love were it not for the wise but extraordinarily difficult command given to the Son for his ultimate glory and honor. This is the hallmark of the Father's love for his Son.

True love, then, is "wrapped" in relationships, and whenever those relationships involve some level of authority and submission, the love of the Son for the Father, and of the Father for the Son, instruct us concerning just what love really is. Our sentimental notions of love need to be displaced with the real-life love shown us in this Father-Son relationship. No greater love exists than this love, and so no better model exists by which we may learn, and relearn, how love is rightly expressed. True love, more often than we think, is shown precisely in loving obedience or in loving authority. May we reflect deeply on the love relationship of the Father and the Son and allow this reality to reshape the love relationships of our lives.

5

BEHOLDING THE WONDER OF THE HOLY SPIRIT

INTRODUCTION

There is one and only one God, eternally existing and fully expressed in three Persons, the Father, the Son, and the Holy Spirit. Each member of the Godhead is equally God, each is eternally God, and each is fully God—not three gods but three Persons of the one Godhead. Each Person is equal in essence as each possesses fully the identically same, eternal divine nature, yet each is also an eternal and distinct personal expression of the one undivided divine nature.

The Holy Spirit, then, is fully God. He is not one-third God, but fully God. Yet, it is not the Spirit alone who is fully God, but he eternally exists along with the Father and the Son, each of whom also possesses fully the identically same divine nature. Because of this, what distinguishes the Spirit from the Father and the Son is not the divine nature of the Holy Spirit. This—the one and undivided divine nature—is also possessed equally and fully by the Father and by the Son. Therefore, what distinguishes the Spirit is his particular *role* as the Holy Spirit in relation to the Father and to the Son and the *relationships* that he has with each of them. In light of both the equality of essence yet differentiation of role and relationship that the Spirit has with the Father and the Son, how, then, may we understand more clearly the distinctiveness of the Holy Spirit in relation to the Father and the Son? In this chapter we shall explore this question, and through this exploration we shall marvel more fully at the wonder that is God the Holy Spirit.

As we focus here on the Holy Spirit, we shine the spotlight on the one who does not seek or desire to be the center of attention. Yet our attention on the Spirit will be in keeping with his own disposition and work, since our focus on the Spirit will expose and magnify his own desire to bring honor to the Son, to the glory of God the Father. So long as we make clear that the Spirit seeks always and only to point away from himself to the Son and, through him, to the Father, we can honor the Spirit in a way that also honors the focus of his own Person and work.

It is nothing short of remarkable that the Spirit clearly embraces and in no respect resents the fact that he has, eternally, what might be called "the background position" in the Trinity. It would be one thing for someone to accept and embrace a background position for a certain period of time knowing that eventually he would be brought out into the spotlight and given more central focus and attention. But here we see something far more amazing, something nearly unbelievable when considered from our perspective as fallen human beings. The Holy Spirit embraces eternally the backstage position in relation to the Father and the Son. As we shall see, even when the Spirit has the role of authority over the incarnate Son, his whole purpose in this work of empowerment and anointing is to advance the work of the Son, to the glory of the Father. Amazingly, even though the Spirit has identically the same nature as the Father and the Son, even though he is fully and equally God, yet he willingly accepts this behind-the-scenes position in nearly everything that the Triune God does. In creation, redemption, and consummation, he willingly accepts the role of supporter, helper, sustainer, and equipper, and in all these respects he forsakes the spotlight. Such is the role of the Spirit within the Trinity, broadly conceived.

Given this, how should we understand, in more specific terms, the Holy Spirit's relationship to the Father and to the Son, and what lessons can we learn for our lives and ministries?

THE SPIRIT ASSISTS IN CARRYING OUT THE WORK OF THE FATHER

Consider with me the humility of the Spirit in relation to the Father by virtue of how he assists the Father's work. While this assistance is true in the creation of the world (Gen. 1:2; Ps. 33:6b) and in the ultimate consummation (Rev. 5:6), the Spirit's assistance is never more apparent than in God's work of the salvation of sinners through the Son.

When one contemplates the Son's coming into the world to accomplish redemption, the Father's role in Christ's coming and work clearly is stressed. As we have considered earlier, it is clear that *the Father sent the Son* into the world to bring about our salvation (e.g., John 3:16; 6:38), and it is also true that the Son sought, in all he said and did, to do only and always *the will of the Father* (e.g., John 8:28-29). Yet, how was the Son enabled to do the work the Father sent him to do? How did he obey, in all that he said and did, the will of his Father? Recall here the words Peter used to summarize the whole of the life and ministry of Jesus, when he spoke about "how God anointed Jesus of Nazareth with the Holy Spirit and with power. He went about doing good and healing all who were oppressed by the devil, for God was with him" (Acts 10:38). This text makes clear what we can observe in many Messianic prophecies and in the Gospel accounts themselves, namely, that Jesus lived his life, resisted temptation, performed his miracles, and in all ways accomplished what the Father sent him to do, through the agency of the Spirit's anointing. The Spirit, then, stands behind the obedience and miraculous power of Christ, and in this Jesus is rendered truly a model for us in our lives, this side of Pentecost.

But notice that Jesus rarely gives "credit," as it were, to the

Spirit for the work and ministry he performs. One example where he does is itself instructive. In Matthew 12, when Jesus had performed a miracle, casting a demon out of a blind and mute man so that he could speak and see (Matt. 12:22), Jesus explained his power to do this as follows: "But if it is by the Spirit of God that I cast out demons, then the kingdom of God has come upon you" (v. 28). Although this text is helpful in indicating the true source of his miraculous power to cast out demons, it is also notable that Jesus' reference to the Spirit was likely because he wanted to call attention to his own identity as the Spirit-anointed Messiah who would bring in the kingdom. In other words, much like Jesus' earlier quoting of Isaiah 61 in Luke 4 when he read Scripture in the synagogue in Nazareth, here likewise, Jesus' reference to the Spirit gives evidence for his own identity. If so, the main reason for mentioning the Spirit was not to give "credit" to the Spirit, per se. Rather, it was to establish clearly who Jesus actually was, in striking contrast to the conclusion the teachers of the law had come to, saying that Jesus cast out demons "by Beelzebul, the prince of demons" (Matt. 12:24).

Apart from this incident and other references to Jesus being filled with the Spirit or led by the Spirit, one looks in vain throughout the Gospel accounts for references to Jesus giving credit to the Spirit for what he did and said. This is true, although both prophets and apostles testify that Jesus carried out his work in the power of the Spirit (e.g., Isa. 11:1-2; Acts 10:38). But this seems not to bother the Spirit at all. Rather, he continues to do his work, behind the scenes, as it were, and assists the Father's calling on the Son's life by enabling him to carry out the mission given him. Without fanfare or accolades, the Spirit simply enables Jesus and seems quite content for Jesus to get the credit and honor. Even in Luke 4, where Jesus had indicated that he was Spirit-anointed by quoting Isaiah 61 to the people in the synagogue, when he finished speaking we read that "all spoke well of him and marveled at the gracious words that were coming from his mouth" (Luke 4:22), yet Jesus did not deflect attention from himself and give it to the Spirit. Nor would the Spirit have wanted him so to do. Rather, the Spirit anointed Jesus with power so that Jesus might be honored in the work he did and words he taught, that the will of the Father might be done.

THE SPIRIT WORKS NOW TO GLORIFY THE SON!

As we have seen, not only does the Spirit assist the Son in carrying out the work of the Father, but more specifically, the Spirit clearly seeks to glorify the Son. Recall the words of Jesus announcing the primary purpose and goal of the Spirit in his coming to indwell and empower his followers: "I still have many things to say to you, but you cannot bear them now. When the Spirit of truth comes, he will guide you into all the truth, for he will not speak on his own authority, but whatever he hears he will speak, and he will declare to you the things that are to come. He will glorify me, for he will take what is mine and declare it to you" (John 16:12-14).

I appreciate J. I. Packer's explanation of this idea in his book, *Keep in Step with the Spirit*. Packer says the role of the Spirit is to mediate the presence of Jesus.[1] So, while the church is under the lordship of Christ, doing his will and obeying his word, the rulership of Christ over his people is exercised as the Spirit works in Christ's followers to "mediate" to them Christ's presence and to move them to honor Christ. As Paul indicates in 1 Corinthians 12:3, the Spirit's role is to promote the lordship of Christ through his presence in our lives. Paul writes, "Therefore I want you to understand that no one speaking in the Spirit of God ever says 'Jesus is accursed!' and no one can say 'Jesus is Lord' except in the Holy Spirit." No one can say, as his heart conviction, "Jesus is accursed," and have the Spirit! And no one can say, as his heart conviction, "Jesus is Lord" except by the Spirit. The Spirit within the believer, then, glorifies the Son. His presence in the lives of individual believers and within the community of faith is not shown by the Spirit making much of the Spirit. Rather the Spirit's presence and work are known as he makes much of the Lord Jesus Christ.

Another passage confirms this same insight. First John 4:1-3 reads, "Beloved, do not believe every spirit, but test the spirits to see whether they are from God, for many false prophets have gone out into the world. By this you know the Spirit of God: every spirit that confesses that Jesus Christ has come in the flesh is from God, and every spirit that does not confess Jesus is not from God. This is the spirit of the antichrist, which you heard was coming and now is in the world already." When the Spirit is present, he puts forward Jesus as the one who has come in the flesh. The Spirit confesses that Jesus is the incarnate Son of the Father who shows us what God is like and gives his life as an atoning sacrifice for sinners. The Spirit bears witness of Jesus, just as Jesus said he would (John 15:26).

With this general principle in mind, that the Spirit comes to glorify the Son, we are prepared to consider more specific ways in which we can see the Spirit lifting up the Son, not himself, in what he does. Consider four aspects of the Spirit's work, each of which gives specific demonstration to the Spirit's deepest longing that the Son be honored.

Special Revelation, Inspired by the Spirit, Focuses on Christ

First, the special revelation that results in Scripture being produced as the inspired Word of God is brought into existence through the work of the Spirit in the minds and hearts of the biblical authors, who then write what is at one and the same time their word and the Word of God—yet their central focus and teaching is on the person and work of the Son. Two passages of Scripture are important for understanding correctly the inspiration of the Scriptures. In 2 Timothy 3:16-17, Paul writes, "All Scripture is breathed out by God [Greek: *theopneustos*] and profitable for teaching, for reproof, for correction, and for training in righteousness, that the man of God may be competent, equipped for every good work." According to Paul, Scripture is the product of God's outbreathing. When the authors write those books that become the thirty-nine Old Testament and twenty-seven New Testament books of the biblical canon, what they write is actually the very Word of God, breathed out through what they write.

But how does it happen that what the biblical authors write is what God wants written? The second passage helps much in explaining this. Concerning Scripture, Peter writes, "Knowing this first of all, that no prophecy of Scripture comes from someone's own interpretation. For no prophecy was ever produced by the will of man, but *men spoke from God as they were carried along by the Holy Spirit"* (2 Pet. 1:20-21). So how is it that we have the Bible that is in fact the Word of God? It is because the Spirit moved the hearts and minds of the writers of Scripture so that when they wrote what they wanted to write—that is, as they wrote the truths that were on their hearts, with the words, grammar, and syntax that they chose to use—the Spirit was working in them so that what they wrote was simultaneously their word and God's Word. This truly is a miracle. We hold that these two things are compatible, namely, that the genuineness of what these human authors chose to write is fully compatible with the work of the Spirit in their minds and hearts ensuring that what they write is nothing other than God's very Word itself. So, "all Scripture is breathed out by God" precisely because "men spoke from God as they were carried along by the Holy Spirit." As Paul reminds believers in another place, "And we also thank God constantly for this, that when you received the word of God, which you heard from us, you accepted it not as the word of men but as what it really is, the word of God, which is at work in you believers" (1 Thess. 2:13). The Bible is God's Word, through human words, as the Spirit works to bring about this God-breathed collection of sixty-six books.

Now, we must ask a question about the primary content and theme of the Bible. Since the Spirit moved the minds and hearts of the biblical writers to write what was also the Word of God, wouldn't it be natural to expect that the result would be a book primarily about the Spirit? That is, since it is true that the Spirit inspired the Scriptures, is it not also true that they primarily are about the one who authored them? Surely, the Spirit who inspired the Scriptures would put himself at center stage, right? Remarkably, as is clear from reading the whole of the Bible in light of the revelation of God in Christ, this simply is not the case. For although the Spirit is primarily responsible for producing the Bible as the inspired Word of God, the Bible is not primarily about the Spirit but rather is primarily about the Son.

Jesus himself made this abundantly clear in what he told various of his disciples after his death and resurrection. You'll recall one incident where Jesus met two of his followers on the road to Emmaus, and he chastened them for their failure to understand things that had been written about him in the Old Testament. When he saw their doubt and lack of faith, he said, "'O foolish ones, and slow of heart to believe all that the prophets have spoken! Was it not necessary that the Christ should suffer these things and enter into his glory?' And beginning with Moses and all the Prophets, he interpreted to them in all the Scriptures the things concerning himself" (Luke 24:25-27). And in similar manner just a short time later with his own disciples, Jesus reinforced this idea that Scripture is mainly about him and his work, for he said to them, "'These are my words that I spoke to you while I was still with you, that everything written about me in the Law of Moses and the Prophets and the Psalms must be fulfilled.' Then he opened their minds to understand the Scriptures" (Luke 24:44-45). So, although the Spirit inspired the Old Testament Scriptures, yet they are primarily about, not the Spirit, but Christ. When Jesus said that he taught his disciples concerning himself from "the Law of Moses and the Prophets and the Psalms," he referred here to the whole of the Old Testament as divided into its three main parts. The Old Testament Scriptures, then, have as their main subject and focus of attention the Messiah, Jesus the Christ.

Is this true of the New Testament also? Perhaps Paul's own perspective will serve to illustrate what ought to be even more obvious, that the New Testament is primarily about Jesus. Paul acknowledges in 1 Corinthians 2 that revelation, inspiration, and illumination are all brought about by the Spirit of God. His focus on revelation by the Spirit is seen in 1 Corinthians 2:6-12, at the end of which passage he says, "Now we have received not the spirit of the world, but the Spirit who is from God, that we might *understand* the things freely given us by God." But not only does the Spirit bring understanding and revelation of the truth itself, the Spirit also works through Paul as he speaks so that the very truths and words he speaks communicating this revelation to others are actually from the Spirit. He continues, "And we impart this [i.e., this revelation] in words not taught by human wisdom but taught by the Spirit, interpreting spiritual truths to those who are spiritual." But the work of the Spirit doesn't end there. Not only does the Spirit reveal truth to Paul, and then provide Paul with the words to communicate these truths to others, the Spirit also works in believers' minds to provide illumination to understand what is taught them. For Paul then also says, "The natural person does not accept the things of the Spirit of God, for they are folly to him, and he is not able to understand them because they are spiritually discerned. The spiritual person judges all things, but is himself to be judged by no one" (1 Cor. 2:14-15). The Spirit of God, then, is responsible, according to Paul, for bringing to him the revelation of truth that he knows (vv. 6-12), for providing him with words to convey this revelation to others (v. 13), and for helping Paul's hearers understand what they hear (vv. 14-16). Revelation, inspiration, and illumination all come from the Spirit.

Given this, it is interesting that if you asked Paul, "What is the content of the preaching and teaching that the Spirit has revealed to you?" his answer would clearly indicate Paul's focus on Christ rather than on the Spirit. For example, Paul writes, "For the word of the cross is folly to those who are perishing, but to us who are being saved it is the power of God" (1 Cor. 1:18). And a few verses later he says, "But we preach Christ crucified, a stumbling block to Jews and folly to Gentiles, but to those who are called, both Jews and Greeks, Christ the power of God and the wisdom of God" (vv. 23-24). Or consider Paul's comment that "I decided to know nothing among you except Jesus Christ and him crucified" (1 Cor. 2:2). And again, "But far be it from me to boast except in the cross of our Lord Jesus Christ, by which the world has been crucified to me, and I to the world" (Gal. 6:14). So, although Paul attributes the revelation, inspiration, and illumination of the truth that he knows, that he conveys, and that believers understand, to the work of the Spirit, at heart this truth itself is about Christ, not the Spirit. Clearly, Paul also speaks about the Spirit, because the Spirit has come to empower the work of Christ in and through his people. But for Paul the central theme is Christ.

The Spirit, then, stands behind the Scriptures. He has inspired them. The Spirit's work in the minds and hearts of biblical authors was the means by which the God-breathed character of the Bible took place. Yes, as we have seen, "all Scripture is breathed out by God" (2 Tim. 3:16) precisely because "men spoke from God as they were carried along by the Holy Spirit" (2 Pet. 1:21). But as the authors of Scripture were moved by the Spirit to write what the Spirit moved them to write, what was the central subject and focus of their writing? Jesus. He's the centerpiece of the Bible. He is what everything points to in the Old Testament, and he is what the New Testament expands upon. All Scripture is given to us by the Spirit. And what the Spirit wants to talk about, most centrally, is Jesus!

Evangelism, Empowered by the Spirit, Proclaims the
Gospel of Christ

According to New Testament teaching, the heart of the gospel, the good news that we have to tell others, is not first and foremost about the Spirit but about the Son. The gospel is the good news of Jesus Christ, "who was delivered up for our trespasses and raised for our justification" (Rom. 4:25). The gospel by which we are saved is this: "that Christ died for our sins in accordance with the Scriptures, that he was buried, that he was raised on the third day in accordance with the Scriptures, and that he appeared . . ." (1 Cor. 15:3-5a). According to Paul, "if you confess with your mouth that Jesus is Lord and believe in your heart that God raised him from the dead, you will be saved" (Rom. 10:9). The gospel, then, is the good news about Jesus Christ—his sinless life, his substitutionary and atoning death, and his victorious resurrection to newness of life—and that by faith in him, we may be saved.

Yet how does this gospel message go out into the world? What means has God devised for people to hear this good news by which (alone) they can be saved? In Acts 1 Jesus told his disciples to wait in Jerusalem for what the Father had promised because, he continued, "you will receive power when the Holy Spirit has come upon you, and you will be my witnesses in Jerusalem and in all Judea and Samaria, and to the end of the earth" (Acts 1:8). The Spirit who Jesus said would bear witness of him (John 15:26) would accomplish this as he empowered these disciples of Jesus to bear witness of Jesus (John 15:27; Acts 1:8). The gospel of Jesus would go forth as the Spirit of Jesus would empower the proclamation of Jesus. The Spirit's focus is necessarily and always on Jesus.

That the Spirit's role, here, is to empower witness to the gospel of Jesus stands in striking contrast to what some evangelicals and others are urging on the church today. There is a growing movement within evangelicalism that would have us think that people outside of the knowledge of Christ and the gospel of his death and

resurrection nonetheless have hope. This movement, often called
"inclusivism," asserts that saving revelation can be brought to the
unreached *by the Spirit* through the created order, and perhaps even
in their non-Christian religions. Thus, these people who have no
knowledge of Christ or the gospel have access, nonetheless, to saving revelation—which is supposedly made available to them by the
Spirit.[2] But what is happening in this model is a separation of
the Spirit and his work from Christ. Inclusivists like this notion
of the Spirit being, as it were, a sort of independent agent, sent from
the Father and not connected to the Son. By this, the Spirit can do
his saving work even though neither the Son nor his gospel is
known. As this theory continues, if these people put trust in the
God made known to them by the Spirit (in creation and, for some,
in other religions), even though they do not know Christ or believe
the gospel, they may be saved—"saved pagans," one might say—
saved, that is, as the Spirit works in them, apart from knowledge of
Christ or the gospel.

In light of this inclusivist proposal, we must examine carefully
what Scripture teaches, and see if there is any kind of independent
work of the Spirit bringing salvation to people, without the Spirit's
bearing witness to Jesus through the Spirit-empowered witness of
Christians who share the gospel. Consider just a few key passages.

Luke 24:46-49. In this passage Jesus said, "Thus it is written,
that the Christ should suffer and on the third day rise from the dead,
and that repentance and forgiveness of sins should be proclaimed in
his name to all nations, beginning from Jerusalem. You are witnesses of these things. And behold, I am sending the promise of my
Father upon you. But stay in the city until you are clothed with
power from on high." Notice several features from this text that
relate to our question.

First, the state of those to whom Jesus sends his disciples is one
of unrepentant sin. This is clear when he says "that repentance and

forgiveness of sins should be proclaimed in his name" to them. Jesus does not view those to whom the gospel is taken as those already forgiven, but rather as those needing forgiveness. They are unrepentant, unforgiven, and unsaved.

Second, the scope of those who are unforgiven, unrepentant, and unsaved is "all nations." That is, Jesus does not see pockets of peoples out there, as the gospel is taken around the world, who are already saved. Rather, this message must be taken from Jerusalem to all the nations, indicating that all the nations need precisely this good news in order to be saved.

Third, the hope for these unsaved in all the nations is precisely that they would repent of their sin as they hear the gospel proclaimed. A proclamation is needed for the unrepentant to be forgiven of their sin and be saved. Apart from the proclamation, they stand in their sin without hope, for apart from the proclamation they do not know what they need to know in order to repent and be saved.

Fourth, the proclamation must be made "in his name" (Luke 24:47), carrying, obviously, the content of the fact that "the Christ should suffer and on the third day rise from the dead" (v. 46). In other words, people must know that Christ has suffered, died, and risen in order to repent of their sin as they hear this proclamation made in the name of Christ. The specific content of the gospel of the death and resurrection is what must be proclaimed and known for people, in all the nations, to be saved.

Fifth and finally, the role of the Spirit is indicated by Jesus when he instructs the disciples to wait in "the city" (Jerusalem) for the "promise" of the Father, until they are "clothed with power from on high." In light of Luke's use of this very same phrase and conception in Acts 1, this clearly is a reference to the empowerment of the Spirit, who when he comes upon them will give them power to be Christ's witnesses, "in Jerusalem and in all Judea and Samaria, and to the end of the earth" (Acts 1:8). The Spirit, then, would empower the disciples when he comes, and as empowered by the Spirit, they then would take the proclamation in the name of Christ to all the nations, in order that people could hear, repent, believe, and be saved by faith in the death and resurrection of Christ. This text teaches powerfully, then, that people must hear the gospel of the death and resurrection of Christ in order to be saved, and that the Holy Spirit was sent precisely to empower this very proclamation in the name of Jesus, that people in all the nations might be saved. The notion that the Spirit works independently of knowledge of Christ and the gospel is directly refuted by Jesus' teaching in this text alone.

Romans 10:1-4, 11-15. Paul expresses his earnest desire and longing for the salvation of his people Israel. "Brothers, my heart's desire and prayer to God for them [Israel] is that they may be saved. I bear them witness that they have a zeal for God, but not according to knowledge. For, being ignorant of the righteousness that comes from God, and seeking to establish their own, they did not submit to God's righteousness. For Christ is the end of the law for righteousness to everyone who believes" (Rom. 10:1-4). Amazingly, Paul's understanding of these fellow Jews is that although they have the Old Testament Law, and even though many have a zeal for God, yet unless they know about Christ, who is the end or culmination of the Law, they cannot be saved. Why is this? Simply because if these Jews are ignorant of the fact that one can be righteous only by faith in Christ Jesus, and if they try to find their right standing before God on their own, they will not be saved. When Paul says that the Jews are "ignorant of the righteousness that comes from God," he means that they are ignorant of the righteousness that comes only by faith in Christ, the "righteousness to everyone who believes." So, as astonishing as it is, Paul sees even these God-fearing Jews who know and endeavor to keep the law of God, as being unsaved apart from faith in Christ. If these Jews are unsaved without Christ, one can only imagine what Paul would say about today's Muslims or Hindus or Buddhists or animists or spiritists who are without knowledge of and faith in Christ. If Jews who have an abundance of special revelation in the Old Testament Scriptures are without hope, of course those who have less revelation from God also are hopeless. What all people need, then, is knowledge of the righteousness that can come only from Christ, who is the "end of the law for righteousness to everyone who believes."

Paul's argument continues that "if you confess with your mouth that Jesus is Lord and believe in your heart that God raised him from the dead, you will be saved" (Rom. 10:9). So, with a logic that is as forceful as it is clear, Paul then says, "For everyone who calls on the name of the Lord will be saved. But how are they to call on him in whom they have not believed? And how are they to believe in him of whom they have never heard? And how are they to hear without someone preaching? And how are they to preach unless they are sent?" (vv. 13-15a). For Paul, it was absolutely clear that people needed to hear the gospel of Christ to believe and call on the Lord to be saved. The Spirit, then, does not work in an independent saving manner apart from the proclamation and knowledge of the gospel of Christ, for it is only by knowledge of this gospel that any can be saved. Since the Spirit has come to glorify Jesus, one central way Jesus is honored is as his person and saving work are made known to Jews and Greeks, for the gospel alone "is the power of God for salvation to everyone who believes" (Rom. 1:16).

Acts 10 and 11. Cornelius is often cited by inclusivists as an example of one who was already saved before he heard the gospel, but who, when he learned of Christ, (also) became a Christian. But is this what Scripture indicates?

Luke makes clear what a pious and God-fearing man Cornelius was before he heard of Christ. Luke tells us that he was "a devout man who feared God with all his household, gave alms generously to the [Jewish] people, and prayed continually to God" (Acts 10:2). But was this devout, God-fearing Cornelius saved? The answer is no. After speaking of Jesus' death and resurrection, Peter said to Cornelius, "And he [God] commanded us to preach to the people and to testify that he [Jesus] is the one appointed by God to be judge of the living and the dead. To him [Jesus] all the prophets bear witness that everyone who believes in him receives forgiveness of sins through his name" (vv. 42-43). Remarkably, as Peter spoke those words—that those who believe in this Christ who has died and been raised are forgiven of their sins—the Spirit descended upon Cornelius and his family, and they were baptized.

Even if the whole account about Cornelius ended here, we would probably conclude that Luke intended that we understand that Cornelius was truly saved at this moment. After all, Peter's sermon clearly indicates that those who believe in Christ are forgiven of their sins. So wouldn't the most likely conclusion be that Cornelius himself, who heard this from Peter at this moment, was forgiven through his own faith in Christ, upon hearing about Christ in Peter's sermon?

But we don't have to guess about this. In Acts 11, Peter reports to those in Jerusalem what had taken place with Cornelius and other Gentiles. And in this report we learn some details that make it clear beyond any shadow of doubt that Cornelius and the Gentiles with him were saved at the time of the preaching of Peter. Notice, for example, that Peter reports what Cornelius had told him: that an angel had appeared to him (Cornelius) and said, "Send to Joppa and bring Simon who is called Peter; he will declare to you a *message by which you will be saved,* you and all your household" (Acts 11:13b-14). Peter then told those to whom he was reporting in chapter 11 that the Holy Spirit fell on Cornelius and the Gentiles just as he had come upon them the Jewish believers at Pentecost. The response of those hearing this report likewise is instructive. They replied to Peter, "Then to the Gentiles also God has granted *repentance that leads to life*" (v. 18).

One more item needs to be pointed out. If we ask what role the Holy Spirit played in this episode, clearly the Spirit came upon Cornelius and the other Gentiles when they believed in Christ and repented of their sin, at Peter's preaching of the death and resurrection of Christ. But there is one more important role played by the Spirit. Peter reports that although he had been reluctant to go to Cornelius (since he was a Gentile), the Lord convinced him that he should go, and then he says, "and the Spirit told me to go with them, making no distinction [i.e., no distinction between Jew and Gentile]" (Acts 11:12). So, the Spirit moved Peter to travel to Caesarea to preach this message by which Cornelius and the other Gentiles would be saved. Yes, the Spirit wants to bring about salvation among the peoples of the world, as shown by the conversion of this first group of Gentiles, but he does it by empowering and sending Spirit-anointed preachers of the gospel, proclaiming what must be heard and known about Christ in order to be saved.

Rather than concluding that Cornelius was saved already because he was devout, and gave of his money to the needy Jews, and prayed regularly to God, instead we draw this sobering conclusion: this description shows just how pious and God-fearing a person can be and yet not be saved. Apart from knowledge of Christ, and apart from faith in Christ who died and was raised for the forgiveness of their sin, people simply cannot be saved, no matter how pious they may be. The Spirit, then, works through the word of the gospel of Christ for the salvation of sinners, and not independent of it.

There is no saving revelation of the Spirit that is not the saving revelation of Jesus Christ and him crucified and risen. Hence, missions is necessary. The hidden peoples of this world are without hope apart from their learning about Christ and placing their faith in him alone for the forgiveness of their sin. We have allowed this concept of the necessity of the spread of the gospel slowly but surely to disintegrate. It's sort of like soap on the floor of the shower. Over time, without being aware of what's happening, it just sits there and vanishes. It gets soft and mushy and after a while it's gone altogether. The Spirit wants his people to know that he has come to empower them to be witnesses of Christ, and that apart from knowledge of and faith in Christ, people cannot be saved. May God grant us emboldened passions to yield to the Spirit, and to see the name of Christ proclaimed by every people, tongue, and nation. Yes, the Spirit has come to glorify Jesus, and this happens in part as the gospel of Jesus reaches the ends of the earth by the power of the Spirit.

Regeneration, Brought About by the Spirit, Brings New Life in Christ

Regeneration to newness of life takes place by the Spirit. Recall Jesus' conversation with Nicodemus:

> Jesus answered him, "Truly, truly, I say to you, unless one is born again he cannot see the kingdom of God." Nicodemus said to him, "How can a man be born when he is old? Can he enter a second time into his mother's womb and be born?" Jesus answered, "Truly, truly, I say to you, unless one is born of water and the Spirit, he cannot enter the kingdom of God. That which is born of the flesh is flesh, and that which is born of the Spirit is spirit. Do not marvel that I said to you, 'You must be born again.' The wind blows where it wishes, and you hear its sound, but you do not know where it comes from or where it goes. So it is with everyone who is born of the Spirit" (John 3:3-8).

Regeneration, or being born again, can happen only as the Spirit of God works in one's heart so as to bring about new life. This is the Spirit's work, to awaken a dead heart (Ezek. 36:26-27; Eph. 2:1) and to open blind eyes (Acts 26:18; 2 Cor. 4:4) so that a person now sees the glory of Christ (2 Cor. 4:6) and responds positively to God, loving what he formerly hated and turning now to the light that he had previously despised (John 3:20-21). Because the condition we all are in apart from this work of the Spirit is one of rebellion against God, we must be made new in order to turn to God in trust and hope. Paul makes clear just how firmly set we are against God in our sin. He writes, "To set the mind on the flesh is death, but to set the mind on the Spirit is life and peace. For the mind that is set on the flesh is hostile to God, for it does not submit to God's law; indeed it cannot. Those who are in the flesh cannot please God" (Rom. 8:6-8). So, as a result of our sinful rebellion and hostility to the true and living God, we cannot put faith in Christ Jesus and we cannot love God.

Paul indicates the same inability to trust Christ elsewhere using a different analogy. To the Corinthians he writes, "The god of this world has blinded the minds of the unbelievers, to keep them from seeing the light of the gospel of the glory of Christ, who is the image of God" (2 Cor. 4:4). Unbelievers cannot see the glory of Christ, much less believe in him. To do so requires the work of the Spirit in their hearts to open blind eyes, to awaken dead hearts (v. 6). This is why the New Testament authors are so jealous that God receive all the glory in our salvation. In our sin we simply cannot take credit for coming to Christ, since we were hostile to God (Rom. 8:6-8), we were blind and unable to see the glory of Christ (2 Cor. 4:4), and we were dead in our trespasses and sins (Eph. 2:1). No wonder Paul exclaims, "For by grace you have been saved through faith. And this is not your own doing; it is the gift of God, not a result of works, so that no one may boast" (Eph. 2:8-9). Our regeneration and conversion, moving us to repent of sin and trust in Christ, is the work of the Spirit. The Spirit must awaken our hearts to see the beauty of Christ, fall before him, and put our hope and trust in him. God gets all the glory in our conversion. And how is Jesus glorified in this? The Spirit awakens our dead hearts and opens our blind eyes to see

Jesus! Amazingly, when the Spirit works in our hearts to bring us salvation, his central purpose is to show us the beauty and glory of Jesus, not himself. Although the Spirit plays this crucial role in our salvation, and even more of a role in our ongoing sanctification (to which we will turn next), nonetheless, his goal is to open our eyes to behold the wonder and glory of Christ (2 Cor. 4:6).

Sanctification, Progressively Achieved by the Spirit, Makes Us More and More Like Christ

Not only does the Spirit reveal and inspire the *word of Christ,* and empower the proclamation of the *gospel of Christ,* and regenerate sinners to behold the *beauty of Christ,* and lead us to place our hope and *faith in Christ,* the Spirit also works mightily in us to conform us more and more into the *likeness of Christ.* This fourth area where we see the Spirit taking the backstage position to both the Father and the Son is in relation to our sanctification. Notice that while Scripture tells us clearly that the Spirit works in believers to bring about their increasing holiness and restoration, the Spirit works not to make the believer into *his* own image but rather into the image of *Christ* (Col. 3:9-10). Sanctification, it is clear, is the work of the triune God. The Father ultimately elected us from before the foundation of the world in order that we would be holy and blameless (Eph. 1:4), and the Father will not fail to bring about our full sanctification (1 Thess. 5:23-24). The Son is equally committed to and sacrificially at work to bring about our purity and holiness (Eph. 5:25-27). But one must ask, How do the Father and the Son bring about our full and final sanctification? And the answer fits all else that we have learned about the *taxis,* the order, within the Trinity. The Father will make us holy as the Holy Spirit works in us to make us like Christ. So again, while the Spirit is the agent sent from the Father ("the promise of the Father," as Jesus indicated in Acts 1:4) to bring his eternal plan to fruition, the Spirit is not the one who receives the honor for this work, first and foremost. The Son is highlighted above the Spirit, since the one in whose image we are remade is the Son, not the Spirit; and the Father receives the ultimate glory, since his purposes and plans stand behind all that is done in our salvation (Eph. 1:3, 6, 12, 14). The Spirit accepts a posture and position of enabling assistance in regard to the work of the Father and the Son, and in this we marvel at his evident humility in relation to both the Son and the Father.

One of the most precious promises and inspiring visions of the work of the Spirit in our sanctification is given us by Paul in 2 Corinthians 3:18. Here he writes, "And we all, with unveiled face, beholding the glory of the Lord, are being transformed into the same image from one degree of glory to another. For this comes from the Lord who is the Spirit." Clearly the Spirit's central focus and unfailing activity is to bring honor and glory to Christ. And here, he does this by working in the lives of believers to transform them increasingly over time so that they are more like what God has saved them to be. But when one asks, Just what is it that God has saved us to be? the answer often given in Scripture is this: God has designed us to be made like his very Son (Rom. 8:29; Col. 3:9-10; 1 John 3:2). The Spirit works in believers, then, to accomplish the work of the Father, to make his children more and more like Jesus his Son.

What does the Spirit do to cause us to be more like Christ? According to 2 Corinthians 3:18, the Spirit focuses our attention on the beauty of the glory of Christ, and by this we are compelled to become more and more like him. Over time, "from one degree of glory to another," the Spirit conforms us increasingly into the likeness of Christ. And of course, this process of becoming like Christ by beholding the glory of Christ began when the Spirit initially opened our eyes in conversion. As we saw earlier, in our sin we were blinded by Satan so that we could not behold the light of the gospel of the glory of Christ, but then God worked to enable us to see the light of his glory in the face of Christ (2 Cor. 4:4-6).

And our final glorification will occur as we behold Christ's majesty and glory, now for the first time unhindered by sin. In that day, at his return, "we shall be like him, because we shall see him as he is" (1 John 3:2). Because God has so made us that we long to become like what we adore, the Spirit helps us see Christ increasingly as glorious and worthy of praise, and when this happens, we seek to become more and more like him. From our initial conversion to our ultimate glorification, the Spirit constantly commends to us the wonder and the glory of the Son. As we see him, aided as we are by the Spirit's illuminating work, we become like him. The Spirit sanctifies us by pointing us to Jesus. The Spirit focuses our attention on Jesus. In our sanctification, as in all of the Spirit's work, he seeks to bring honor and glory to the Son, to the ultimate glory of the Father.

Confirmation of this very understanding of the Spirit's work, to make us like Christ to the glory of the Father, can be seen in Paul's prayer for the Ephesian believers at the end of Ephesians 3:

> For this reason I bow my knees before the *Father,* from whom every family in heaven and on earth is named, that according to the riches of his glory he may grant you to be strengthened with power through his *Spirit* in your inner being, so that *Christ* may dwell in your hearts through faith—that you, being rooted and grounded in love, may have strength to comprehend with all the saints what is the breadth and length and height and depth, and to know the love of *Christ* that surpasses knowledge, that you may be filled with all the fullness of God (Eph. 3:14-19).

Notice in particular Paul's prayer that these believers may be "strengthened with *power through his Spirit*" in their inner beings "*so that Christ* may dwell" in their hearts through faith. For Paul, the very presence and power of the Spirit in the lives of believers provides the basis and enablement for their transformation. But just what exactly will this transformation accomplish, by the Spirit's empowerment? The Spirit will work in such a way that Christ will dwell or abide more fully in their hearts as they put their faith firmly in him. As we have seen everywhere else, so it is true here, that the Spirit promotes Christ, not himself. And Paul clearly understands this. He prays for the Spirit to work so that *Christ's presence* may be enlarged in them, as it were, so that they will comprehend in increasing measure "the *love of Christ* that surpasses knowledge." The Spirit, then, enlarges the likeness of Christ and expands the experience of Christ in the lives of those who put faith in Christ. The Spirit, in short, glorifies Christ in our sanctification.

Yet notice one more detail. Paul begins his prayer bowing his knees neither to the Son nor to the Spirit but to the Father, "from whom every family in heaven and on earth is named." The Father, then, is the sovereign Ruler over heaven and earth, controlling even the very names that every creature is given. From this position of sovereign supremacy, it is the Father who has the authority to grant this prayer's fulfillment, and so ultimately all glory and thanksgiving must go to him. Because of this, Paul prays to the *Father* that the *Spirit* will enlarge the likeness and experience of *Christ* in those who believe. As Paul's prayer so clearly indicates, then, the Spirit works in our sanctification to bring honor and glory to the Son, to the ultimate glory of the Father.

THE SPIRIT TAKES THE THIRD POSITION, AFTER THE FATHER AND THE SON, IN THE AGE TO COME

Finally, in the age to come, the Spirit will take the backseat to the Son and the Father. What has been true in eternity past, in the incarnation of the Son upon the earth, and through all of the work of the Father and the Son in our lives now as Christ builds his church, is also true in eternity future, as the Spirit takes the position subordinate to both the Son and the Father. Consider one indication of this. Revelation 5 offers a glorious vision of worship that will take place at the end of the age when the Lamb, who was worthy to break the seals and open the book, along with the one on the throne, is worshiped. Halfway through this vision we read,

> And between the throne and the four living creatures and among the elders I saw a Lamb standing, as though it had been slain, with seven horns and with seven eyes, which are the seven spirits of God sent out into all the earth. And he went and took the scroll from the right hand of him who was seated on the throne. And when he had taken the scroll, the four living creatures and the twenty-four elders fell down before the Lamb, each holding a harp, and golden bowls full of incense, which are the prayers of the saints. And they sang a new song, saying, "Worthy are you to take the scroll and to open its seals, for you were slain, and by your blood you ransomed people for God from every tribe and language and people and nation, and you have made them a kingdom and priests to our God, and they shall reign on the earth." Then I looked, and I heard around the throne and the living creatures and the elders the voice of many angels, numbering myriads of myriads and thousands of thousands, saying with a loud voice, "Worthy is the Lamb who was slain, to receive power and wealth and wisdom and might and honor and glory and blessing!" And I heard every creature in heaven and on earth and under the earth and in the sea, and all that is in them, saying, "To him who sits on the throne and to the Lamb be blessing and honor and glory and might forever and ever!" And the four living creatures said, "Amen!" and the elders fell down and worshiped (Rev. 5:6-14).

The Spirit is in this vision, but clearly he takes the backstage, behind-the-scenes position. The Spirit is alluded to in verse 6 when the Lamb is said to have seven eyes "which are the seven spirits of God sent out into all the earth." Here, the Spirit is pictured as "seven eyes" which are "seven spirits," giving the Spirit the number of perfection. This is the perfect Spirit, the Spirit of God. And the Spirit as the "seven spirits" is sent out "into all the earth" indicating his role, on behalf of the Son, in bringing in people from every tribe, language, people, and nation. Just as the Son (i.e., the Lamb slain) was given to ransom "people for God from every tribe and language and people and nation" (5:9), so the Spirit had been sent out into all the world on behalf of the Son, presumably, to bring in those ransomed and saved by the Son. So the Spirit is in this text, but he is in the supporting role we have come to see as the normal position of the Spirit.

And while the Spirit is represented in this passage in a veiled and subtle way, it is the Son and the one on the throne, his Father, who receive primacy in worship. When the elders and the living creatures throughout heaven and earth fall down in worship, they cry out, "To him who sits on the throne [the Father] and to the Lamb [the Son] be blessing and honor and glory and might forever and ever!" (Rev. 5:13), but they say nothing of the Spirit. The Spirit willingly takes the behind-the-scenes position. He is present and even central in bringing to faith those who worship the Lord as the redeemed, but he is not up front being honored. The Spirit, then, while being eternally God and while possessing the identically same nature as the Father and the Son, willingly and eternally takes the position of supporter, helper, assistant, and behind-the-scenes worker, always pointing attention to the Son, to the ultimate glory of the Father.

APPLICATION FROM THE ROLE OF THE SPIRIT IN RELATION TO THE FATHER AND THE SON

1. Be instructed by the Spirit's deep and abiding willingness to serve unnoticed, without overt recognition, without singled-out honor.

Though the Holy Spirit is God, equal in essence to the Father and the Son, yet his role is consistently to defer honor, to seek to bring about the glory of another. Imagine that. It is *always* the role

of the Spirit to bring honor to the Son, to the ultimate glory of the
Father. Do you think there may be a lesson in this for us? We can
find it difficult, even on a temporary basis, to be the behind-the-
scenes person who is not recognized. There is something in all of
us that wants to be seen and to receive the credit for what we've
done. To accept the behind-the-scenes position where no one may
know and notice the service we have rendered is difficult indeed. To
work sacrificially, all for the purpose of pointing constantly to
another, and for the honor he might receive, can be extremely hard
to accept. But this is the way of the Spirit, and this is the power that
is at work in us, to help us to serve to the honor of Christ, that he
may receive *all* the glory. When this happens, it will not be of our
doing; our flesh resists this at every step. But it helps enormously
to realize that this not only is our calling, to the glory of our Lord
and Master, but it is the eternal role and delight of the Spirit of God;
and this Spirit indwells us to give us his power so to live.

2. Ponder the Spirit's willingness to assume authority over the
    incarnate Son.

Even though the Spirit is given authority over the incarnate
Son, so that the Son follows the lead of the Spirit and performs his
miracles in the power of the Spirit, nevertheless the Spirit knows
that this authority is not permanent. And he knows that this authority is not over the eternal Son of the Father, but only over the Son
incarnate. And furthermore, he knows his role in this authority and
leadership is ultimately not for the sake of honoring himself, but for
the honor of the Son who carries out the will of the Father. The
Spirit assumes this authority over the incarnate Son and assists the
Son in glorifying the Father. It's all about the honor of the Son to
the glory of the Father, and the Spirit accepts this gladly. In seeing
this, we should marvel that even when the Spirit is given a delegated
authority over the Son, he does not use it in a manner that puts him-

self first. He recognizes that, even here, he is third. He is, after all, assisting the work of the Son by which every knee will bow and every tongue will confess that Jesus Christ is Lord, to the glory of the Father (Phil. 2:10-11). Yet, in all of this, there simply is no hint of jealousy, no bitterness, no resentfulness; rather, the Spirit exhibits nothing but loving, caring, willing, joyful service.

3. Marvel at the Spirit's willingness to surrender his authority over the incarnate Son, as the Spirit is sent, at Pentecost, from the Father and the Son.

After the Spirit has completed his work of empowering the incarnate Son to fulfill the will of his Father, he is sent into the world at Pentecost from the Father *and* the Son. Yet the Spirit doesn't begrudge the fact that the Son, along with the Father, now has authority over him. The Son, with the Father, sends the Spirit into the world, and the Spirit gladly glorifies the very Son over whom he has previously (even if temporarily) had authority. This is so contrary to how we think and behave as human beings and sinners. We might accept the fact that we're told to do something by one who clearly is our boss. But if an "equal" who is under the authority of that same boss were to tell us to do something, we might well cringe.

And notice the difference between the Son and the Spirit in this respect. The Son said constantly that he came from heaven to do the will of his *Father,* and that the *Father* had sent him into the world. There is no mention of the Spirit here as involved in the sending of the Son. And yet, when the Spirit comes into the world, it is so clear that even though the Spirit proceeds from the Father, he also is sent from the Son (John 15:26; Acts 2:33). Yet, although the Spirit is sent from both the Father *and the Son,*[3] he shows no resentment. The Spirit accepts this role. He embraces it. He joyfully, willingly takes the position of being third—all the time third.

4. Marvel at the harmony and unity of the love relationship within the Trinity.

Yes indeed, marvel at the social relationship of joy, fulfillment, love, and unity among the members of the Trinity. There is no bickering, no fighting, and no disputing who has the right to do such and such. There is nothing but mutual support for the respective roles that each eternally has. And in those differing job descriptions of the three divine Persons, there is unity and harmony of purpose, joy, peace, love, fulfillment, and full satisfaction. We must here resist the lie of our culture that says the only way that we can exist happily together is if we always and only acknowledge everyone as exactly the same. Unity is not sameness, and harmony requires differences working together. If we want a wonderful example of this, we need only look at the Trinity. We should be astonished that while there is sameness in terms of the identical divine nature possessed fully by all three, there also is differentiation in terms of individual Person and relationship and role. But in and through both the sameness of nature and the distinction of Person and role there is joyous harmony, peace, and love within the Trinity.

Can marriages be like this? Can a husband accept his place as head of the home, and a wife accept her place, submitting to her husband, while both recognize their equality of human nature and work for a joyous harmony in their relationship? Can it happen in churches as congregations recognize that there is a qualified male leadership, designated by God, while all in the congregation are equal members of the body of Christ, working together with various gifts and abilities, all for the unity of the faith? May God help us. And may we be inspired and empowered by the Spirit. What a beautiful case study in humility the Spirit is. What a beautiful example of willingness to accept the behind-the-scenes place for the sake of advancing the common mission, unified purpose, all for the glory of another. May we marvel at the wonder that is this Spirit, the Spirit of the living God.

6

BEHOLDING THE WONDER OF THE TRIUNE PERSONS IN RELATIONAL COMMUNITY

INTRODUCTION

Christians have long affirmed that there is one and only one God, yet there are also three equal, eternal, and individual personal expressions of the one undivided and eternal nature of the one God. The Father, Son, and Holy Spirit are each fully God, each equally God, each possessing fully the one undivided divine nature. Yet each Person of the Godhead is different in role and position in relation to each other. The Father is supreme in authority, the Son is under the Father, and the Spirit is under the Father and the Son. Yet there is also full harmony in their work, with no jealousy, bitterness, strife, or discord.

Clearly, when we behold the Trinity for what it is, we stand amazed. We are astonished at the unity and harmony of their common work in and through the authority-submission relationship that marks their roles and responsibilities for all eternity. Unity of purpose and harmony of mission, yet with differentiation in lines of authority and submission within the Godhead—this truly is a marvel to behold.

Given what we have seen in this study, what lessons can we take away for our lives and churches? Of course, we have anticipated some answers to this question already. But here we will reconsider some wonderful ways to apply what it means to be the people of God, made in the image of God, created and called to live our lives as reflections of this our Triune God.

LESSONS FOR OUR LIVES AND MINISTRIES FROM THE RELATIONSHIPS AND ROLES OF THE TRIUNE GOD

1. God intends that his very nature—yes, his triune and eternal nature—be expressed in our human relationships.

What does it mean to be created in the image of God? Certainly, scholars and Bible readers over the centuries have affirmed that whatever "image of God" is, it is vital and central to our understanding of what it means to be human. As we read the story of creation in Genesis 1, we see "let there be" and similar words over and over. "Let there be light," "let there be an expanse," and so forth. But in verse 26, with the creation of man, it all changes. Here we read, "Then God said, 'Let us make man in our image, after our likeness" (Gen. 1:26). There is an intentionality expressed in these words, indicating that man, more fully than any other part of creation, will reflect and represent what God is like. Although the heavens declare God's glory (Ps. 19:1), only man is made in God's image.

While some have thought of "image of God" primarily in structural ways (i.e., aspects of our nature that render us God's image) and others have seen the image of God as our relationships with God or others, one thing that Genesis 1:26-28 emphasizes is that the man and woman God creates in his image are commanded to "rule over" or "subdue" the other aspects of the created order. I follow the insights of D. J. A. Clines and A. A. Hoekema that the image of God has to do primarily with

how we are to live our lives as God's representatives, carrying out
his will and "ruling" on his behalf.[1] While I've argued for this
understanding elsewhere, this definition of image of God con-
ceives of both male and female as:

> created and finite *representations* (images *of* God) of God's own
> nature, that in *relationship* with Him and each other, they
> might be His *representatives* (imaging God) in carrying out the
> *responsibilities* He has given to them. In this sense, we are
> *images of God* in order *to image God* and His purposes in the
> ordering of our lives and carrying out of our God-given
> responsibilities.[2]

If we are thus to represent God and reflect who he is in our relationships and activities, part of this involves reflecting the ways in
which the triune Persons relate to one another. As we see the love
relationship among the Trinitarian Persons, we should seek the
same kind of love to be expressed among us, God's people. And as
we see the harmony expressed amidst differing roles and responsibilities among the members of the Trinity, we should seek this
same kind of harmony as we acknowledge varying gifting and activities within the body of Christ. And, as we see thoughtful, judicious
authority exercised along with joyful, glad-hearted submission
within the very Trinity itself, we should seek to exemplify these
same kinds of qualities in our relationships of authority and submission. In short, we should look not only to the character of God,
and to the commands of God, but also to the triune roles and relationships among the Triune Persons of God to see what it means
to live our lives as his images. We are created to reflect what God
is like, and this includes a reflection of the personal relationships
within the Trinity.

2. Eternal relationality calls for and calls forth a created community of persons.

The very fact that God, though singular in nature, is plural and societal in person, indicates that we should not view ourselves as isolated individuals who happen to exist in close proximity to others, but as interconnected, interdependent relational persons in community. It is not enough just to exist together alongside but independent of others, along the lines of how a lot of guys live in a dorm—sharing space with other guys whom they just pass in the hall or see across the room. They exist in close proximity, perhaps, but is there really a relationship of community in many such cases? God intends that there be a created community of persons in which there is an interconnection and interdependence, so that what one does affects another, what one needs can be supplied by another, and what one seeks to accomplish may be assisted by another.

Isn't this true in the Trinity? We have seen over and again that what one member of the Trinity does affects another. The interconnectedness and interdependence among the members of the Trinity is such that one is hard-pressed to think of any "work of God" which does not involve various members of the Trinity working together. For example, God the Father designs what the purpose of the created order will be. In this, he designs that his Son be the one who comes and redeems sinners. The Father designs it, but his fulfillment of that design depends upon the Son obeying the Father. And yet the Son obeying the Father depends upon the Spirit empowering the Son. There is an interdependence, an interconnection intrinsic to the very nature of God.

Living in isolation with the pretense of autonomy is, of course, "the American way." Our heroes are those rugged individuals like the Lone Ranger or Superman or Rambo who can do everything themselves and need no one's help. But when we insist on going solo, when the "I did it my way" syndrome strikes, we are essentially rejecting God's plan for how we should live with one another. When we refuse to be in relationships of accountability and interdependence with one another, we are choosing to live in violation of God's created design. It's really that simple.

So, look at the Trinity and *think again* about what it means to be human. Yes, the relationships in the Trinity call for and call forth a created community of persons. We need to think very hard about this in our churches. It is one of the reasons a small group ministry is such a good thing. Small groups are one key way in which we can establish, in our churches, communities of interconnection and interdependence. Surely this is also one of the main reasons that the Spirit assigns gifts to each believer in the body of Christ, so that we will both give to one another and depend on one another in our growing in Christ. Interconnection and interdependence are key themes we see in the Trinity that we need to see lived out increasingly in our lives and churches. Let's give thoughtful and prayerful attention to building Trinity-like communities of interdependence and interconnection with one another, working with each other, for each other, and doing so with harmony and love for one another.

3. The relationships in the Trinity exhibit so beautifully a unity that is not redundancy, and a diversity that is not discord.

Consider again the difference between unison and harmony in music. Unison achieves a kind of unity, but without texture and with built-in redundancy. With unison, you have several voices singing the same melody. And while unison has its own beauty, there is in harmony a kind of glorious unity with texture and complexity that is simply lacking with unison. The unity achieved through harmony avoids redundancy, for every voice matters, and every part contributes its unique sound. The beauty of harmony is a beauty of diversity without discord, of distinctiveness without disarray, of complexity without cacophony.

While only an analogy, the contrast between unison and harmony helps reflect something true of the Trinity. Here, we have a three-part harmony in which each "Voice" sings the same song, following the same composition and reading off the same page, yet each Voice joyfully sings a different part, and the three together contribute a richness and texture that no one voice alone could accomplish.

In our own relationships in the home and in ministry, we should endeavor, by God's grace, to model our work and worship in ways that reflect the trinitarian unity expressed through harmony. This will mean, on the one hand, that we celebrate rather than begrudge many of the differences among us. When we insist that everyone be just like "me," we have settled for the unity of unison and we have lost the vision of harmony. Rather than bemoan the fact that God gives various gifts in the body of Christ, and rather than look down on others whose interests in ministry and service vary from our own, we can see these as the harmonious display of various "voices" which, if they sing correctly, can create a beautiful common song. Our differences, so long as they are within the boundaries of the moral character of God and express the gifting of the Spirit, need to be embraced and employed in Christian service, both in the home and in the church.

On the other hand, work and worship that reflect the trinitarian unity expressed through harmony will also seek to follow one conductor and to sing or play off the same score of music. When the differences among us result in each person doing what is right in his or her own eyes, we have moved from harmony into the pain and hurt of anarchy. Harmony works only with differences that are fettered by common cause. Our various parts must be played or sung according to what the common music of the whole choir or orchestra calls for. We must all be seeking to follow the same leader and make our contributions in ways that assist the whole. In the Trinity, the various parts played by the Father, Son, and Holy Spirit lead to the beauty and unity of harmony, and this is the model we should emulate in our relationships.

4. The most marked characteristic of the trinitarian relationships is the presence of an eternal and inherent expression of
   authority and submission.

*Both authority and submission are good, for both are expressive of God
himself.* This principle is about as countercultural as we can imagine,
though some will simply dismiss it as old-fashioned. But it is the
truth.

We live in a culture that despises authority at every level.
Whether the authority of police, or of government, or of parents,
or a husband's authority in marriage, or pastoral authority in our
churches—our culture has programmed us to despise authority. We
find it hard to think positively about authority for one very simple
reason: we are sinners who want to be in charge of our own lives.
We want to be captains of our own destiny. We want to govern our
own futures. And here, one of the lessons of the Trinity is that God
loves what we despise; namely, God loves, exercises, and embraces
rightful authority-submission relationships. God loves this
authority-submission structure because God embodies this very
structure in his trinitarian relations of Persons. If we have difficulty
embracing authority and submission, we can be helped by two
things: 1) recall that it is our own sinful urge for independence that
leads us to despise authority and want our own way; and 2) reflect
on the fact that in the very eternal relations that are true of the
Persons of the Trinity, authority and submission are lived out with
love and joy. We must learn to embrace what is eternally true in
God, and this means, among other things, embracing rightful
authority and rightful submission.

If our homes and our churches are truly to be countercultural,
we need to exhibit a whole-hearted, healthy respect for authority.
Imagine how your coworkers will notice if you exhibit a respect for
authority and a heartfelt desire to follow through with what you've
been instructed by your boss to do. Imagine how husbands will

notice when their wives submit with joy and gladness to the husband's leadership in the home. Imagine how much better it will be for our children if they are raised in homes where they know that the authority of their parents must be respected; and as they learn to obey with joy at home, they will learn to obey God with this same joy. The fact is, one of the most remarkable single feature in this relational community that we call the Trinity is this presence of authority and submission. So, if we are to model our lives after the nature of God, we must learn joyfully to embrace both rightful authority and rightful submission.

5. Equality of essence does not conflict with distinction of roles. In God, and among us, both must be embraced and honored.

Advocates of the egalitarian view often argue that if you believe that God has designed in creation a distinction in roles among his human creation, with male leadership in the home and the church, then you cannot avoid the conclusion that men are superior to women, and women are inferior to men.[3] But I would suggest that this clearly is not the case, for two reasons.

First, one can see by analogy to other relationships that a distinction in authority and submission does not entail one's superiority and the other's inferiority. Take parents and children. Surely we must hold that parents have authority over their children and children are to obey their parents (Eph. 6:1-3). But is it not also clear that parental authority does not make parents superior to their children or children inferior to their parents? Both parents and children are fully human, fully made in the image of God, and fully deserving of the dignity and rights accorded to all human beings. Some children may even be more intelligent or physically fit than their parents, but they still are commanded to submit to their parents. What is true here could be said of any number of other relationships where authority and submission are involved. Distinction in role does not indicate distinction in value.

Second, the clearest example of how the egalitarian argument fails is in relation to the Trinity. The commonality and equality of nature shared by the Father, Son, and Holy Spirit is even greater than the commonality of nature shared by two human beings. For in the Trinity, the Father, Son, and Holy Spirit each possesses the identically same divine nature. There are not three natures, but one; there are three Persons, each of whom possesses the identically same divine nature fully and eternally. And yet there are eternal role distinctions among the members of the Trinity. Therefore, just as the role distinctions characterized by relationships of authority and submission do not compromise the complete equality of the triune Persons of the Godhead, so is this the case with us, who are made in God's image. Men and women are fully equal in essence, worth, value, and dignity, even though God has ordained that there be male headship in our relations in the home and in the church. Equality of essence does not conflict with distinction of roles. In God, and among us, both must be embraced and honored.

6. Trinitarian roles and marriage: both equality of essence of male and female, and distinction of husband and wife roles, are designed by God and are reflective of the Trinity.

It is clear from Genesis 1:26-27 that God created "male and female" in his image, and hence both are created equal in their humanity, dignity, worth, and value. But it is also clear from Genesis 2 that in the very creation of the man and then the woman, God established the headship of the man over the woman. Some, of course, deny this. They say that there is no reason to think from Genesis 2 that God intends male headship in the relationship of the man and the woman. All he does is create one first, and then the other, in order to show that both are needed to fulfill his design for them. But there is no male authority indicated in Genesis 2, they would say.

There are many problems with this view, but the most obvious problem is that Paul sees things differently. In two passages, 1 Corinthians 11:5-10 and 1 Timothy 2:12-15, Paul makes the point that women should recognize male authority in certain settings *because* God's very creation of the man and the woman indicates that male headship was part of God's design in creation. For example, in both passages, Paul refers to the simple fact that it was Adam who was created first, not the woman (1 Cor. 11:8; 1 Tim. 2:13). So evidently it mattered that God created the man first and the woman second. Evidently God's point was not only to indicate that both are needed to fulfill what God intends for them, but also that in this relationship, the man has headship or authority, since the priority of the man over the woman is shown through his being created first. Further, in 1 Corinthians 11:9 Paul indicates that the man was not created for the woman's sake but rather the woman was created for the man's sake, and because of this, women should recognize male authority in the Christian community. Male headship, then, is part and parcel of the very created design of God for men and women, and this reflects something of God's very triune nature.

What can men and women, respectively, learn from this? Permit me to suggest two applications for husbands and fathers, and two for wives and mothers.

Two applications for husbands and fathers. First, married men and fathers need to realize and embrace the truth that God has invested in them a special responsibility for spiritual leadership in relation both to their wives and children. Husbands and fathers bear responsibility for the spiritual nurture of their homes, a responsibility that is just not the same for wives or other members of the household. Heads of households are granted both the privilege and duty, before the Lord, to lead in the spiritual direction, training, and growth of their wives and children.

This is abundantly clear as it relates to the spiritual well-being of both a husband's wife and a father's children. No clearer or more forceful passage could be mentioned here than Ephesians 5:25–6:4. A husband is called to regard his relationship with his wife as being like Christ's relationship with the church. As Paul reminds us, Christ loves the church dearly and deeply and gives himself for her "that he might sanctify her, having cleansed her by the washing of water with the word, so that he might present the church to himself in splendor, without spot or wrinkle or any such thing, that she might be holy and without blemish" (Eph. 5:26-27). Then Paul adds these words: "In the same way husbands should love their wives as their own bodies" (v. 28). We simply could not ask for a more forceful or more compelling directive to husbands concerning their responsibility as spiritual leaders and lovers for their wives. The gravity of the husband's responsibility toward his wife is perhaps best captured in Paul's statement of the end goal of Christ's love toward the church: "that she might be holy and without blemish" (v. 27). The husband, then, must take to heart his sober and joyous responsibility to long and work and love and pray for the continual spiritual growth of his wife. One of the greatest problems in our Christian culture today is that husbands are simply not encouraged to think in this way. But since marriage is meant by God, from the beginning, to be a reflection of Christ's relationship with his church (vv. 31-32), husbands have the rich opportunity and privilege to "model Christ" before others as they exercise loving authority over their wives in a manner reflective of Christ's loving lordship over the church. Just as there is rightful authority and submission in the Trinity, husbands must accept and embrace this God-given mandate to undertake leadership in the spiritual growth of their wives.

Continuing in this passage, we see that Paul tells children to "obey [their] parents in the Lord for this is right." They are to "'honor [their] father and mother,'" for "this is the first commandment with a promise" (Eph. 6:1-2). Notice that "parents"—that is, both the father and the mother—are in view in these first two verses; children are to obey their "parents" and they are to honor their "father and mother." So, one might expect that in the next verses, Paul would continue to address both parents in relation to his next command. But he doesn't. Rather, he now offers his direction specifically to the fathers of the household. As he writes, "Fathers, do not provoke your children to anger, but bring them up in the discipline and instruction of the Lord." The point is clear: *Fathers* in particular bear special responsibility for the spiritual growth of their children. As heads of their houses, they could abuse their authority in ways that would provoke their children to anger. But instead, they are to create an atmosphere where they lead their children in the discipline of obedience to Christ and in learning the teaching and wisdom of Christ. Fathers have both the God-given mandate and the privilege of blessing their children by cultivating a home environment where children grow to respect, love, obey, and follow Christ, in obedience to their fathers and in honor of both their fathers and mothers.

In both relationships of headship—husbands' headship over their wives, and fathers' headship over their children—we must constantly be aware of our two main sinful tendencies. One sinful response of a person in the position of headship is to abuse that position by being heavy-handed, mean-spirited, harsh, and demanding in unloving and selfish ways. God has not given men this authority in our homes for the purpose of gratifying our own pleasures and exploiting the opportunity for our ease and comfort. Rather, such authority must be exercised out of benevolence. A position of headship must be used to promote healing, life, restoration, growth, prospering, and joy. A second sinful response to our position of headship, though, is far more insidious yet far less obvious. We may

respond to God's call to exert leadership in our homes by abdicat-
ing our responsibility. We are not mean-spirited; rather, we're just
not there. We are apathetic, distant, often absent, and altogether
uninterested and uninvolved in the spiritual direction of our wives
and children. The harm we inflict on our homes through such apa-
thy and uninvolvement can be as painful and wounding as the harm
inflicted through heavy-handed selfishness. Here, our wives wilt
before our eyes, and our children grow distant as they become more
and more attached to peers in a quest for the love, affection, and
leadership they lack from their fathers. In both cases, though, husbands and fathers have lost sight altogether of what true biblical
headship is to mean for our homes.

The well-being of those under our charge must occupy our
thoughts of what it means to be granted this position of authority
over them. Husbands and fathers, then, are given a stewardship and
a responsibility that attaches to their positions as heads of their
homes, and they must seek, by God's grace and strength, to bring
about spiritual growth and well-being for their wives and children.
The relations of authority and submission in the Trinity call us to
realize that God intends homes to reflect the reality that is true in
the Godhead itself. May God be merciful and restore to Christian
husbands and fathers the joyous vision of both the privilege and
responsibility of being heads of their homes, for the spiritual well-
being of our wives and children.

Second, men must realize that their position as heads of homes
in no way indicates their supposed superiority over their wives, in
particular, or over women, in general. First Peter 3:7 could not be
clearer regarding how God views a husband who thinks or acts in a
demeaning manner toward his wife. Peter writes, "Likewise, husbands, live with your wives in an understanding way, showing
honor to the woman as the weaker vessel, since they are heirs with
you of the grace of life, so that your prayers may not be hindered."
In all likelihood, the reason egalitarians think that male authority

necessarily entails female inferiority is simply that they've seen this lived out in concrete cases of marriages and homes. While it is not true, as argued above, that male headship requires a view that women are inferior, nonetheless many husbands communicate this very wrongheaded idea to their own wives.

Peter reminds us here of the truth, however. Notice how he links together both the submission of the wife (stressed, of course, in 1 Pet. 3:1-6) and the full equality of the man and the woman. Yes, she is the weaker vessel; and yes, the husband must work at understanding her needs, recognizing that she is different from him. However, says Peter, show her honor at the same time! Recognize that she, with you, is an heir of the grace of life in Christ, so that she, with you, possesses all the riches of Christ and shares fully in being made into the likeness of Christ. Just as the man and the woman are created equal in the image of God (Gen. 1:27), so in Christ, a believing man and a believing woman are fully equal in all the spiritual blessings and riches of Christ (1 Pet. 3:7b; Gal. 3:28). Husbands must regard their wives with honor and respect, or, God warns, he will not attend to their prayers. So, male headship in our homes is real and important. Husbands and fathers are to plan and work and pray that they may lead their wives and children into new vistas of spiritual understanding and growth. But they must also respect their wives as fully equal, with them, in all that they possess in Christ. Equality of essence and differentiation of role—these realities need to be lived out in our homes as they are eternally expressed in the Trinity.

Two applications for wives and mothers. First, every New Testament passage offering instruction directly to wives includes one common element: in every case wives are commanded to submit to their husbands (see Eph. 5:22-24; Col. 3:18; Titus 2:3-5; and 1 Pet. 3:1-6). It seems rare any longer even at Christian weddings that the bride's vow will include the promise to "submit to" or "obey" her husband. We live in a culture that despises submission as much as it despises authority, but God calls us to a different mind and heart on this matter. And here, wives can benefit enormously from the doctrine of the Trinity in realizing that the submission required of them as wives is itself reflective of the very submission eternally given by the Son to his Father, and by the Spirit to the Father and the Son. In this sense, God calls wives to be what he *is,* just as he has also called husbands to be what he also *is.* Therefore, in obeying Scripture's command that wives submit to their husbands, it is not enough before God simply to grit your teeth, buck up, and say, "Okay, if you insist, God, even though I don't like it and I don't want to do it, I'll submit."

Why is such begrudging submission insufficient? It is insufficient in part because it fails to understand the nature of submission as reflective of the Son's submission to the Father, and the Spirit's submission to the Father and the Son. In the Trinity, just as the Father takes his responsibility of authority seriously and exercises it with impeccable wisdom and goodness, so the Son and Spirit render joyous and glad-hearted submission, always longing to do just what is asked or commanded of them. In addition, begrudging submission also fails because it does not express what a wife's submission to her husband is meant to reflect, according to Paul in Ephesians 5. Just as the husband's thoughtful and loving headship reflects Christ's relationship to the church (Eph. 5:25-27, 31-32), so the wife's glad-hearted and consistent submission reflects the church's responsibility and privilege of absolute submission before the lordship of Christ (Eph. 5:24, 31-32). Therefore, the kind of submission a wife is to render to her husband needs to be a joyful, heartfelt, willing, glad-hearted submission. A wife, then, should seek before God to render submission that longs to help, longs to serve, and longs to assist in any way that will be an encouragement to her husband. Just as God calls all of us to submit to authority with a whole heart and willing spirit, so this special calling and privilege is given to wives, to the honor of Christ and his church, and as a reflection of the triune relations within the Godhead.

Second, submission can be very difficult. Unlike the church's relationship before Christ, where the church can be confident that anything that Christ commands of the church will be both wise and for its good, husbands cannot be counted on to lead with such flawless wisdom and goodness. In fact, sometimes husbands are pitifully unlike Christ, and submission can be very, very difficult. Wives are not commanded to "retrain" their husbands, though they might endeavor to do so through godly example and fervent prayers. But, despite husbands' sinfulness and failures, wives nonetheless are commanded to submit to these imperfect husbands.

The most striking passage here is Peter's instruction to wives. Peter specifically addresses wives whose husbands are unbelieving. Presumably, these husbands may be the most difficult for a Christian wife to live with and under. As a general rule, anyway, an unbelieving husband would have far less in common with his wife's spiritual interests and may make it more difficult for her to live as a Christian. Despite this, Peter instructs these wives to be subject to their own husbands, so that even though their husbands do not believe, they may be won to Christ by the godly conduct of their wives (1 Pet. 3:1-2). It is surely amazing that this text, relating as it does to a Christian wife of an unbelieving husband, contains stronger language on the wife's submission than any other New Testament passage on husband-wife relations. As Peter commends to these wives of unbelieving husbands the importance of living before their husbands with a gentle and quiet spirit, he appeals to Sarah as an example. Peter says that Sarah "obeyed Abraham, calling him lord" (v. 6a), indicating that Christian wives would be Sarah's "children" if they followed this example without fear (v. 6b).

So, submission may be very difficult in many cases for Christian women. The husbands of some Christian wives are not responsible and loving in the ways God commands them to be. Furthermore, no Christian husband will love his wife perfectly; every husband will fail in many ways. Yet faithfulness to God's Word calls us to uphold the importance and necessity of wives submitting with gladness, even to difficult husbands, even in difficult marriages. With faith and hope, they should pray for God to work in their husbands' lives. Of course, we all recognize that there may be times, in extreme cases, when the wife's or children's well-being is threatened because of an abusive husband. In such cases, other biblical principles come to bear that would justify a wife separating from her husband for a period of time in order to seek the protection, the healing, and the restoration that are needed. And yet, while such measures must be taken in some cases, for most wives, while they are not responsible to "change" their husbands, they are responsible before God to submit to them, even when it is not easy to do so. The husband, of course, is responsible before the Lord for his own character and conduct as a husband, and he will give an account. But the Christian wife is responsible for herself and for her attitudes and responses to her husband. So I urge Christian wives: make your relationship to your husband an issue of spiritual accountability before the Lord, and live before your husband in a way that honors Christ. Remember, God will honor you as you seek to honor him and his Word. He will bless you enormously as you seek to obey him by being faithful to fulfilling what he has called you to do. May God help us to see that Trinitarian roles and relationships are meant to be reflected in marriage as both husbands and wives manifest what is true eternally in the very triune nature of God.

7. Trinitarian roles and the church: both equality of essence and distinction of roles are designed by God to be expressed among pastoral leaders and congregations, and this dynamic is reflective of the Trinity.

It is both significant and telling that just prior to Paul discussing why women should manifest by their very attire that they recognize male headship (1 Cor. 11:4-16), he introduces the discussion with this assertion: "But I want you to understand that the head of every man is Christ, the head of a wife is her husband, and the head of Christ is God" (1 Cor. 11:3). Role relations between men and women, generally, and role relations in the church, particularly, are important according to Paul because they are meant to reflect the more ultimate realities of Christ's headship over mankind, and the Father's headship over Christ. Can we not see from this that the current despising of male authority in pastoral leadership positions in the church undercuts and undermines the very design God has intended for the church? Just as marriages are to reflect Christ and the church, so churches are to reflect the Father's relationship to Christ and Christ's authority over mankind. First Corinthians 11:3 sets the discussion of male and female roles in the believing community in this broader and glorious framework of God and Christ, and Christ and mankind.

So why should women have their heads covered when they pray or prophesy (vv. 4-16)? Such covering, says Paul, is a symbol of the authority invested in the male leadership of the church (v. 10). Rather than despising or denying the God-invested authority in our churches, Paul calls us to recognize and symbolize this very authority structure. Only some men are qualified to lead the church as elders and pastors (1 Tim. 3:1-7); other men, and all women, must follow their leadership. But, because here it is women who submit precisely because of their gender, they are called to demonstrate their recognition of male authority in a symbolic fashion. Male headship applies not only to marriage but equally in the church, where qualified elders, who are male, are those who rightly serve in leadership positions.

This is confirmed, of course, in 1 Timothy 2:12, where Paul says, "I do not permit a woman to teach or to exercise authority over a man; rather, she is to remain quiet." Paul's instructions in 1 Corinthians 11 are simply reaffirmed here, to a different church. Because God has granted the right to serve as elders or pastors in the church only to qualified men (1 Tim. 3:1-7), so also he prohibits women from the two main activities and duties involved in being an elder or pastor. Women may not "teach" and they may not "exercise authority" over men. That is, they are not to take up those responsibilities that are given, by God's design, to qualified men.

Notice here that it might have been natural for Paul to have said, in 1 Timothy 2:12, "I do not permit a woman to be an elder." After all, he is just about to discuss qualifications of elders that include their being "able to teach" (1 Tim. 3:2) and to "manage his own household well" and to "care for God's church" (vv. 4-5). Since elders are responsible to "teach and exercise authority" in the church, Paul could easily have said that he did not permit a woman to be an elder. But he does not say exactly that. Instead, Paul focuses on the distinctive elder *functions* of teaching and exercising authority, not the *office* of elder, per se.

This is instructive, it seems to me. Many of the questions that arise today, regarding whether it is appropriate for a woman to serve in some capacity or another, can be helped if we see this. For example, what about women teaching a mixed male-female adult Sunday school class? Would that be appropriate? After all, she isn't preaching on Sunday mornings, nor is she one of the pastors of the church. So would this be in accord with Scripture's own boundaries of what a gifted and able woman could do? In answer to this (and other similar cases), it helps much to recall that Paul did *not* say that he forbids women from being elders, per se. Now, of course, he does forbid this (see 1 Tim. 3:1-7 and Titus 1:5-9, where elders clearly are male), but this is not how he puts it. Rather, Paul specifies the distinctive functions that qualified men alone are to carry out, namely, "teaching" and "exercising authority" over men. So, it seems clear that a woman should not teach a mixed male-female adult Sunday school class, since to do so would involve her "teaching" men, even if it did not involve her being a pastor of the church. That is, even though an adult Sunday school teacher may not be a pastor (or elder), nevertheless the teacher would be doing something that only qualified men should do.

Perhaps a principle derived from this example may help with other such questions. When we consider the appropriateness of a woman serving in some ministry capacity that did not exist in the New Testament church, we could ask the question, "Is this contemporary ministry position sufficiently 'elder-like' to warrant applying elder principles and so allowing only a qualified man to serve in it?" To give just one more example, I serve as a professor of theology in an evangelical seminary, and one of my main duties is to teach men and women the glorious truths that make up the body of our Christian beliefs. Now, I ask myself the question, Is the position of theology professor at a seminary sufficiently "elder-like" to warrant applying elder principles, so that only a qualified man should serve in this position? I believe the answer clearly is yes. I think particularly of Paul's statement in Titus 1:9 regarding an elder, that "he must hold firm to the trustworthy word as taught, so that he may be able to give instruction in sound doctrine and also to rebuke those who contradict it." This verse comes pretty close to comprising my job description as a theology professor! And to think that I have the responsibility of teaching the "faith that was once for all delivered to the saints" (Jude 3) to many young men who will then pastor churches and teach in other institutions, passing on to their congregations and classes the truths God has given me the privilege to teach them—yes, I believe that my role, though it didn't exist in the New Testament when Paul wrote 1 Timothy 2 and 3, is sufficiently "elder-like" to require that only qualified men, and not women, be considered to be professors of theology.

So, as with marriage, our roles in the church are meant to display both the equality of essence and the distinction of roles present, eternally, in the Trinity. As the Son submits eternally to the Father, and as the Spirit submits to the Father and the Son, so we are to reflect this same reality in our marriages and our churches. There should not be chafing or resentment but rather an acceptance and embrace of the good design of God, reflecting his own nature in the authority-submission structures he has designed.

And remember, not only does submission in the church relate to the role of women in ministry; it applies to all men and women alike who sit under the authority of those qualified men who pastor and lead our churches. Hebrews 13:17 speaks to all church members, saying, "Obey your leaders and submit to them, for they are keeping watch over your souls, as those who will have to give an account. Let them do this with joy and not with groaning, for that would be of no advantage to you." What an enormously important statement this is for us in our churches. Men and women alike should view pastoral leaders as something more than merely the dispensers of good advice or even of divine wisdom. They surely are this, but they are more. These pastoral leaders are, in fact, called and designated by God to lead their people in spiritual growth. Much like the responsibility husbands and fathers have in their homes, so pastoral leaders in churches must keep watch "over the souls" of those in their care. And, as Hebrews 13:17 indicates, we assist pastors and elders in carrying this out by our submissive and receptive attitudes. We benefit most, and they enjoy the greatest fulfillment, when we recognize rather than resist the God-ordained order of pastoral leadership of our churches, comprised by qualified and gifted men of God.

8. Trinitarian roles and prayer: the *taxis* eternally present in the Trinity, of Father, Son, and Holy Spirit, in this order, forms the framework for meaningful, biblical prayer.

In a very telling and instructive comment, Paul writes, "For through *him* [Christ] we both have access in one *Spirit* to the *Father*" (Eph. 2:18). It's a short verse, and very simple, to be sure, but what it teaches speaks volumes about the Trinity and its relation to prayer. First, notice that we have access "to the Father." That is, our prayers should be directed, as Jesus himself taught us, to "Our Father in heaven" (Matt. 6:9). The Father is the supreme authority over all, for even the exalted Son, who reigns over heaven and earth, sits at the right hand of the Father (Eph. 1:20), and the Father has put all things in subjection under the Son's feet (vv. 21-22; 1 Cor. 15:27-28). Earlier in Ephesians Paul gave specific praise to "the God and Father of our Lord Jesus Christ" (Eph. 1:3) for his blessing us with every spiritual blessing we enjoy, all of which comes to us through his Son. The Father, then, as supreme authority over even his own Son and the Spirit, is the one to whom we gladly, but humbly, address our prayers.

Second, our prayers are to be extended to the Father "through" his Son, our Lord Jesus Christ. For it is through Christ and Christ alone that saved Jews and Greeks alike have their common access to the Father. Christ is the "one mediator between God and men, the man Christ Jesus," as Paul puts it in 1 Timothy 2:5. So, we rightly pray to the Father but we come "in the name" of the Son, or by his very authority. We recognize that we are able to come into the presence of God only because we come in Christ's authority, as those clothed in him. As we read in Hebrews, "we have confidence to enter the holy places by the blood of Jesus, by the new and living way that he opened for us through the curtain, that is, through his flesh, and since we have a great priest over the house of God, let us draw near with a true heart in full assurance of faith, with our hearts sprinkled clean from an evil conscience and our bodies washed with pure water" (Heb. 10:19-22). Christ, then, is our only access to the Father, and so we come in his name, by his atoning work, to the very throne room of grace where the Father awaits those now clothed with the righteousness of his Son.

Third, on the question of the Spirit's relation to prayer, Paul writes that Christians should be "praying at all times in the Spirit, with all prayer and supplication" (Eph. 6:18). For recall that through Christ, we have our access *in one Spirit* to the Father (Eph. 2:18). Prayer is to be "incited," as it were, by the Spirit. The Spirit moves within our hearts and assists us in bringing our prayers and petitions to the Father, in the name of the Son. Prayer is in the power of the Spirit, as he empowers all else that we do to the glory of Christ in our lives.

Prayer, then, follows a paradigm that reflects the *taxis* of the Trinity. The Father has absolute and uncontested supremacy, including authority over the Son and the Spirit, so we pray to the Father. Yet we cannot come to the Father on our own; we have no right of access as finite creatures and as sinners. So we come only on the basis of Christ, the one who alone is Mediator between God and men. We come in the name of Jesus. We come by his authority, and because of his grace. As we pray, "In Jesus' name, Amen," at the end of our prayers, these are anything but throw-away words! This makes the difference between a prayer that reaches the Father and empty, vain words. So we come to the Father, in the name of Jesus, but we are able to come only in the power of the Spirit. We need the Spirit within us, conforming us more and more to the likeness of Christ, to help us pray those things that are in keeping with the will of Christ. Christ is Lord, and the Spirit honors the lordship of Christ by assisting us to pray what furthers and fulfills Christ's very kingdom work. We must pray, then, at all times "in the Spirit." Christian prayer takes its lead from the doctrine of the Trinity, in recognition of the eternal *taxis* reflected in the trinitarian relations among the Persons of the Godhead. Christian prayer, as such, is prayer to the Father, in the name and by the authority of the Son, in the power of the Holy Spirit.

9.   Trinitarian roles and worship: the *taxis* eternally present in the Trinity, of Father, Son, and Holy Spirit, in this order, forms the framework for meaningful, biblical worship.

Two passages from Paul's letter to the Philippians are helpful here. Paul indicates that believers in Christ are really the true expressions of new covenant life and transformation, and as such, he says, they are "the real circumcision, who *worship by the Spirit of God* and *glory in Christ Jesus* and put no confidence in the flesh" (Phil. 3:3). The connection between the two concepts of worshiping in the Spirit and of glorying in Christ should not be missed. When the Spirit of God works within us to promote worship, the one result that must surely come is that those so worshiping by the Spirit will give great glory to Christ Jesus their Lord. In keeping with what we have seen earlier of the Spirit's chief mandate and passion to bring glory to the Son (John 16:14), here we see that the Spirit is the one who inspires worship within us, but that just as surely, the worship he elicits is focused on the Son. New covenant believers, those who have the Spirit, are those who are enabled truly to worship. But because the Spirit within them, the Spirit who enables their worship, is the Spirit who comes to glorify Jesus, therefore the Spirit works within their hearts so that they express the honor, majesty, greatness, glory, and grace of Christ in their worship.

If we now consider what Paul had said earlier about the worship that will take place one day in the future when every knee will bow before Christ, we learn one more element that is so helpful and instructive. Recall that Paul spoke of this day, when Christ will stand before every creature in heaven and earth as the exalted Lord, and every knee will bow and every tongue will confess "that *Jesus Christ is Lord,* to the *glory of God the Father*" (Phil. 2:11). While the Spirit elicits worship of the Son—for all proclaim that "Jesus Christ is Lord"—nonetheless, all worship of the Son, in and of itself, is penultimate. That is, worship of the Son, while right and true and glorious, must also recognize the one whom the Son himself acknowledges as supreme over all, even over himself. The ultimate object of our honor, glory, praise, and worship is the Father of our Lord Jesus Christ, who himself alone is over all. Just as the Son himself will one day "be subjected to him [the Father] who put all things in subjection under him, that God [the Father] may be all in all" (1 Cor. 15:28), so we must recognize even now that all worship to the Son, while Spirit-inspired and Spirit-wrought, is always meant also to reverberate yet further to the glory and majesty of the Father.

And this is as both the Son and the Father will it to be! The Son takes such great delight in constantly giving credit and honor to his Father. All that the Son does, he tells us over and again, is to fulfill the will of the Father and is for the glory of his Father. Yet the Father takes such delight in revealing himself in his fullness through his Son, so that the very character of the Father is manifested fully in his Son. The Son, then, as the "radiance of the glory of God and the exact imprint of his nature" (Heb. 1:3), is the very Son in regard to whom the Father commands, "Let all God's angels worship him" (v. 6). Because the Father's glory is reflected in the Son (cf. John 1:14), the Father takes delight in pointing attention to his Son. "Worship my Son!" the Father would say to all; "Through the Spirit who proceeds from me, be empowered to worship him," he commands. Yet, because the very character and glory of the Son is the character and glory of the Father, all worship of the Son must redound to the glory of the Father. Hence, Christian worship must be worship of the Son, by the power of the Spirit, to the ultimate glory of the Father. Worship is deeply satisfying and correctly expressed to the glory of this triune God only as it is exercised within this trinitarian framework.

10. Because God eternally exhibits both full equality of essence and rich diversity in role, we can be confident that both are good.

God is good. His ways are good. And his design for human life and relationships is good. And here we see from the doctrine of the Trinity that both equality of essence and differentiation of role are good. Just as God is in himself one in essence, and that one essence is possessed equally, fully, infinitely, and eternally by the Father, the Son, and the Holy Spirit, so we cherish the reflection of this reality as God created man as male and female, both fully and equally in his image. But that's not all. Just as God is in himself three in person, so that Father, Son, and Holy Spirit are each individual personal expressions of the one undivided divine essence, and each relates to the others according to an eternal *taxis* or order of authority and submission within the Godhead, so we cherish the reflection of this reality as God created authority-submission structures as his purposeful design for many kinds of human relationships. That the God who is one in essence and three in person is also good, enables us to accept and embrace the equality and differentiation, and the authority and submission, that by God's design are part and parcel of our own human existence. God is good, and his ways are good. Given this, we will experience the joy and satisfaction of human life only when we embrace, not resist, his created design. And as this good and wise created design is lived out in human relationships, as wives and husbands, as congregations and elders, as people living with one another in community, we can be confident that when we live out what God is like we will enter into the good that he has designed for us to know. To the glory of the triune God, may we learn to embrace the manifold ways that God has designed human life to reflect the wonder and glory of the God who is eternally one and three.

CONCLUSION

Throughout much of evangelical Christianity, the doctrine of the Trinity has been neglected. While we profess to believe that God is one, and that each of the Persons of the Godhead is fully divine, yet we have missed out on so much. We have not been reading our Bibles—particularly our New Testaments—sufficiently through "trinitarian glasses," and we have not devoted ourselves to the meditation and study required to understand better just what the revelation of God as Father, Son, and Holy Spirit means. Our brief study is a small step toward helping some among us to become more aware of the richness and the glory that are conveyed in understanding God as he is, the one God who is Father, Son, and Holy Spirit.

In particular, we have wondered at the relationships and roles that each of the divine Persons has with the others. In unique and remarkable ways, each member of the Trinity relates distinctively with the other members, yet each contributes in ways that advance and fulfill the one common plan and purpose of God. The unity of the Godhead is seen in that each of the three divine Persons possesses the identically same nature simultaneously, fully, and eternally; and all of the divine Persons work together in absolute harmony to support one another in accomplishing the common divine task, from creation to the new creation and beyond. Yet this unity of nature and purpose is expressed through the three individual and distinctive Persons of the Godhead, with each member setting about his own work joyful to labor and support and yield and command, according to the eternal *taxis* that is intrinsic to the life of triune God. Whether submitting, serving, and obeying, or whether leading, sending, and commanding, each divine Person accepts his respective roles and responsibilities with complete and unabashed delight. The eternal authority and submission structure of the Trinity does not permit deviation, so that authority and submission are themselves eternal realities. While the Father embraces and revels in his position of being supreme in the Trinity, so too do the Son and Spirit embrace and revel in their positions as second and third, respectively. No competition, no jealousy, no bitterness, and no dispute exist among these Persons. Here in the Trinity, rather, we see hierarchy without hubris, authority with no oppression, submission that is not servile, and love that pervades every aspect of the divine life. Unity and diversity, identity and distinction, sameness and difference, melody and harmony—these are qualities that mark the rich texture of the life of the one God who is three.

To understand God as triune is also to see more clearly what creaturely life is meant to be. Our study of the Trinity opens a window to examine more carefully a part of the design for human relationships. For here we see that the divine unity and diversity, identity and distinction, melody and harmony, are meant by God to be reflected in finite though genuine expressions among us in human relationship. As God is one, so human beings are created in that one image, fully human and fully equal. Yet, as God is three—and particularly by virtue of the eternal *taxis* that orders the relations of the divine Persons—so human beings must embrace the created *taxis* of their human relations. Equality exists alongside authority and submission in human life, as God has designed it to be. We will find joy and fulfillment only when we embrace, not repel, this very design. Oh how we can learn what it means to live life as creatures in the image of God as we observe God living life as a Trinity of Persons.

With deep gratitude and humility before God, we acknowledge how far we have to go, both in understanding God as he is, and in living life as God meant this to be. By his grace, may both our vision for God and our longing for living life aright be enhanced, as we see more clearly the beauty and glory of the one God who is three. And so, to the Father, and to the Son, and to the Holy Spirit, we give praise, honor, and glory, both now and forevermore. Amen.

NOTES

Chapter One
Beholding the Wonder of Our Triune God:
Importance of This Doctrine

1. All Scripture quotations are from the English Standard Version of the Bible. All emphases in these quotations were added by the author.

Chapter Two
Beholding the Wonder of Our Triune God:
Historical Overview

1. For more thorough discussion of the development of the doctrine of the Trinity in the early church, see J. N. D. Kelly, *Early Christian Doctrines,* rev. ed. (San Francisco: HarperSanFrancisco, 1978); and Jaroslav Pelikan, *The Emergence of the Catholic Tradition (100–600),* vol. 1 of *The Christian Tradition: A History of the Development of Doctrine* (Chicago: University of Chicago Press, 1975).

2. Paul often uses "God" for the Father, specifically. So, here, it is clear that he speaks of the Father by his use of "God," and he does not for a moment mean to indicate that the Son and the Holy Spirit are not God. The benediction form of this statement demonstrates otherwise. Paul's way of saying "May God be with you" is "May Father [God], Son, and Spirit be with you." For further discussion of Paul's common usage of "God" for the Father specifically, along with Paul's deliberate use of *theos* (Greek: "God") for Jesus Christ, see Murray J. Harris, *Jesus as God: The New Testament Use of "Theos" in Reference to Jesus* (Grand Rapids, Mich.: Baker, 1998).

Chapter Four
Beholding the Wonder of the Son

1. For further discussion of the eternal authority-submission relationship within the Trinity, with particular focus on the relationship of the Father and the Son, see J. Scott Horrell, "Toward a Biblical Model of the Social Trinity: Avoiding Equivocation of Nature and Order," *Journal of the Evangelical Theological Society* 47/3 (September 2004): 399-421; and Wayne Grudem, *Evangelical Feminism and Biblical Truth: An Analysis of More Than 100 Disputed Questions* (Sisters, Ore.: Multnomah, 2004), chapter 10.

2. By "freedom" I do not have in mind here the use of this word as it relates to discussions of "the freeodm of the will" or of what constitutes "volitional freedom," per se. Rather, in this context (following John 8:31-32), "freedom" refers to human life lived at its best, or to the kind of human living that brings the greatest joy and satisfaction. For a discussion of "the freedom of the will" or the true nature of "volitional freedom," see Bruce A. Ware, *God's Greater Glory: The Exalted God of Scripture and the Christian Faith* (Wheaton, Ill.: Crossway, 2004), 78-95.

3. See, e.g., Gilbert Bilezikian, "Hermeneutical Bungee-Jumping: Subordination in the Godhead," *Journal of the Evangelical Theological Society* 40/1 (March 1997): 57-68; Stanley J. Grenz, "Theological Foundations for Male-Female Relationships," *Journal of the Evangelical Theological Society* 41/4 (December 1998): 615-630; Royce G. Gruenler, *The Trinity in the Gospel of John: A Thematic Commentary on the Fourth Gospel* (Grand Rapids, Mich.: Baker, 1986); and Millard Erickson, *God in Three Persons: A Contemporary Interpretation of the Trinity* (Grand Rapids, Mich.: Baker, 1995).

4. Some egalitarians acknowledge the eternal inner-trinitarian Father-Son relation yet do not understand this as implying or entailing relations of authority and submission in the created order. See Craig Keener, "Is Subordination Within the Trinity Really Heresy? A Study of John 5:18 in Context," *Trinity Journal* 20 NS (1999): 39-51.

5. See, e.g., Thomas R. Schreiner, *1, 2 Peter, Jude,* vol. 37 of The New

American Commentary (Nashville: Broadman & Holman), 87-88. Schreiner comments, "In the Greek text of v. 19 the word 'Christ' appears last, separated from the term 'blood' by five words. The text was likely written in this way so that it would be clear that the Christ was the subject of the participle commencing v. 20. The Christ 'was chosen before the creation of the world'" (87).

6. For a discussion of evidence that early church theology upheld the simultaneous eternal equality of essence yet functional relationship of authority and obedience among the Persons of the triune Godhead, see also Robert Letham, "The Man-Woman Debate: Theological Comment," *Westminster Theological Journal* 52 (1990): 65-78; and Stephen D. Kovach and Peter R. Schemm, Jr., "A Defense of the Doctrine of the Eternal Subordination of the Son," *Journal of the Evangelical Theological Society* 42/3 (September 1999): 461-476. In limited space, Kovach and Schemm cite examples from Hilary of Poitiers, Athanasius, the Cappadocian fathers, and Augustine, with supporting commentary from John Calvin, Philip Schaff, Jaroslav Pelikan, J. N. D. Kelly, Charles Hodge, and W. G. T. Shedd, and they cite (471) the conclusion of Paul Rainbow, "Orthodox Trinitarianism and Evangelical Feminism," 4 (unpublished paper, based on his dissertation, "Monotheism and Christology in 1 Corinthians 8:4-6" [D.Phil. diss., Oxford University, 1987]), in which Rainbow concludes, "From the earliest form of the creed we can see that the Father and the Son are united in being, but ranked in function."

7. Augustine, *The Trinity,* trans. Edmund Hill, vol. 5, *The Works of St. Augustine* (Brooklyn: New City, 1991), IV. 27 (emphasis added).

8. See, e.g., Paul K. Jewett, *Man as Male and Female: A Study of Relationships from a Theological Point of View* (Grand Rapids, Mich.: Eerdmans, 1975), 71.

9. P. T. Forsyth, *God the Holy Father* (1897; reprint, London: Independent Press, 1957), 42.

10. P. T. Forsyth, *Marriage, Its Ethic and Religion* (London: Hodder & Stoughton, 1912), 70-71.

11. John Thompson, *Modern Trinitarian Perspectives* (New York: Oxford University Press, 1994), 22.

12. Colin E. Gunton, *The Promise of Trinitarian Theology*, 2nd ed. (Edinburgh: T & T Clark, 1997), 197.

Chapter Five
Beholding the Wonder of the Holy Spirit

1. J. I. Packer, *Keep in Step with the Spirit* (Old Tappan, N.J.: Revell, 1984), 49. Packer writes, "The distinctive, constant, basic ministry of the Holy Spirit under the new covenant is to mediate Christ's presence to believers . . .".

2. Some key inclusivist defenses include Clark H. Pinnock, *A Wideness in God's Mercy: The Finality of Jesus Christ in a World of Religions* (Grand Rapids, Mich.: Zondervan, 1992); and John Sanders, *No Other Name: An Investigation into the Destiny of the Unevangelized* (Grand Rapids, Mich.: Eerdmans, 1992).

3. The Western church adapted the Nicene Creed to say, in its third article, that the Holy Spirit proceeds from the Father "and the Son" (*filioque*) and not merely that he proceeds from the Father (alone). While I agree fully with this additional language, I believe that this biblical way of speaking, as found in John 15:26, refers to the historical sending of the Spirit at Pentecost and does not refer to any supposed "eternal procession" of the Spirit from the Father and the Son. The conceptions of both the "eternal begetting of the Son" and "eternal procession of the Spirit" seem to me highly speculative and not grounded in biblical teaching. Both the Son as only-begotten and the Spirit as proceeding from the Father (and the Son) refer, in my judgment, to the historical realities of the incarnation and Pentecost, respectively.

Chapter Six
Beholding the Wonder of the Triune Persons
in Relational Community

1. I discuss the history of this doctrine and recent developments in Bruce A. Ware, "Male and Female Complementarity and the Image of God,"

in Wayne Grudem, ed., *Biblical Foundations for Manhood and Womanhood* (Wheaton, Ill.: Crossway, 2002), 71-92.

2. Ibid., 79.

3. One of the first proponents of this argument was Paul K. Jewett. See his *Man as Male and Female: A Study of Relationships from a Theological Point of View* (Grand Rapids, Mich.: Eerdmans, 1975), 69-82.

GENERAL INDEX

SCRIPTURE INDEX

Titus

1:5-9	149
1:9	150
2:3-5	144

Hebrews

1	33
1:1-2	33
1:2	34
1:3	33, 34, 155
1:6	34, 155
1:8	34
1:10-12	35
2:8	47
4:15	75, 94
5:8	93
5:9	93
9:14	39, 99
10:19-22	152
13:8	35
13:17	151

James

1:13	53
1:17	53
2:19	28

1 Peter

1	78
1:18-21	78
1:20	101

1:21	79
2:21-22	91
3:1-2	146
3:1-6	144
3:6	146
3:7	143, 144

2 Peter

1:20-21	109
1:21	112

1 John

3:2	124
4:1-3	108
4:10	54

Jude

3	150

Revelation

5	125
5:6	105, 126
5:6-14	126
5:9	127
5:13	84, 127
19	47
19:13	47
19:16	47